ANTARCTIC ADVENTURE

by Sir Vivian Fuchs

Illustrated with maps, line drawings and 16 pages of full-colour photographs

Sir Vivian Fuchs has written the exciting story of his great journey across Antarctica. Twelve men and eight vehicles with sledges and dog teams set out from Shackleton Base to cross more than 2,000 miles of unexplored snow and ice. When these men, along with Sir Edmund Hillary, reached Scott Base on the far side of the continent, the explorer's dream of a land crossing of Antarctica had at last come true.

Sir Vivian describes the incredible adventures that he and his comrades went through—the crossing of crevasses which almost engulfed both men and vehicles; the terrible punishment inflicted by miles of serrated, iron-hard ridges of ice; the blinding "whiteouts" which deprived the travellers of all sense of direction; the climbing of ice precipices and unknown mountain ranges; the perils of running out of fuel in the middle of the freezing wilderness.

Stirring and fast-paced, here is a true story of courage and endurance that will thrill and inspire the young reader.

D1159881

Antarctic Adventure

The Commonwealth

Trans-Antarctic Expedition 1955-58

Antarctic

The Commonwealth Trans-Antarctic Expeditio

Illustrated by Stuart Tresilian

Adventure

by Sir Vivian Fuchs

E. P. Dutton & Company, Inc., New York

Author's Acknowledgements

In the writing of this book, as with its elder brother, *The Crossing of Antarctica*, I have been indebted to all the members of the expedition for their whole-hearted assistance at all times. It is natural that much of the information I have incorporated was derived from the accounts of others, both in the field and at home.

I would particularly like to thank Sir Edmund Hillary for the information about the Ross Sea Party; Kenneth Blaiklock, Roy Homard, and Peter Jeffries, for details of life at Shackleton during the first winter, and John Lewis who provided the story of the Trans-Polar flight.

Finally, I wish to acknowledge the help given by Mrs. Eleanor Honnywill of our London office, whose suggestions throughout the preparation and correction of this book have been invaluable.

V. E. F.

The Commonwealth Trans-Antarctic Expedition 1955-58

Expedition Leader: Dr. Vivian Fuchs.

1955–1957 ADVANCE PARTY (M.V. *Theron*)

K. V. Blaiklock, *Leader. Surveyor.*
R. A. Lenton, *Deputy leader. Carpenter and radio operator.*
R. H. A. Stewart, *Meteorologist.*
P. H. Jeffries, *Meteorologist.*
J. J. La Grange, *Meteorologist* (South Africa).
Sergeant-Major D. E. L. (Roy) Homard, R.E.M.E., *Engineer.*
Sergeant E. (Taffy) Williams, R.A.F., *Radio operator.*
Dr. R. Goldsmith, *Medical officer.*

1956–1958 TRANS-POLAR PARTY (M.V. *Magga Dan*)

*Dr. V. E. Fuchs, *Leader. Geologist.*
*D. G. Stratton, *Deputy leader. Surveyor.*
K. V. Blaiklock, *Surveyor.*
*D. L. Pratt, *Engineer.*
Sergeant-Major D. E. L. (Roy) Homard, R.E.M.E., *Engineer.*
R. A. Lenton, *Carpenter and radio operator.*
J. J. La Grange, *Meteorologist* (South Africa).
J. G. D. Pratt, *Geophysicist.*
Dr. A. F. Rogers, *Medical officer and physiologist.*
Dr. H. Lister, *Glaciologist.*
Dr. P. J. Stephenson, *Geologist* (Australia).
*W. G. Lowe, *Photographer* (New Zealand).

Royal Air Force Contingent
*Squadron-Leader J. H. Lewis, *Senior pilot.*
*Flight-Lieutenant G. M. Haslop, *Second pilot* (New Zealand).
*Flight-Sergeant P. Weston, *Aircraft mechanic.*
Sergeant E. (Taffy) Williams, *Radio operator.*

1956–1958   ROSS SEA PARTY   (H.M.N.Z.S. *Endeavour*)

*Sir Edmund Hillary, *Leader.*

*J. H. (Bob) Miller, *Deputy leader. Surveyor.*

Lieutenant-Commander F. R. Brooke, R.N., *Surveyor* (Great Britain).

R. A. Carlyon, *Surveyor.*

Dr. R. W. Balham, *Meteorologist and biologist.*

B. M. Gunn, *Geologist.*

G. Warren, *Geologist.*

Dr. G. W. Marsh, *Medical officer and in charge of dogs* (Great Britain).

M. H. Douglas, *Mechanic.*

M. R. Ellis, *Engineer.*

J. E. Gawn, *Radio operator.*

Chief Petty Officer P. D. Mulgrey, R.N.Z.N., *Radio operator.*

H. H. Ayres, *Mountaineer.*

J. G. Bates, *Mechanic and carpenter.*

E. S. Bucknell, *Cook.*

Royal New Zealand Air Force Contingent

*Squadron-Leader J. R. Claydon, *Senior pilot.*

Flying-Officer W. J. Cranfield, *Second pilot.*

Sergeant L. W. Tarr, *Aircraft mechanic.*

  * Accompanied the Advance Party in the *Theron,* returning in February 1956.

MEMBERS OF THE NEW ZEALAND I.G.Y. PARTY
WHO SHARED SCOTT BASE

Dr. T. Hatherton, *Leader. Geophysicist.*

V. B. Gerard, *Geophysicist.*

W. J. P. MacDonald, *Technician.*

R. H. Orr, *Technician.*

H. N. Sandford, *Radio mechanic.*

Contents

Contents

Illustrations

The reader may feel that the selection of colour photographs between pages 80 and 81, and pages 112 and 113, are a somewhat romantic interpretation of the colouring in Antarctica. I would like to emphasize, therefore, that the colours seen may be both varied and vivid according to the season and the time of day. These pictures taken by George Lowe and Jon Stephenson give an excellent idea of the colours as they really are.

Maps and Plans

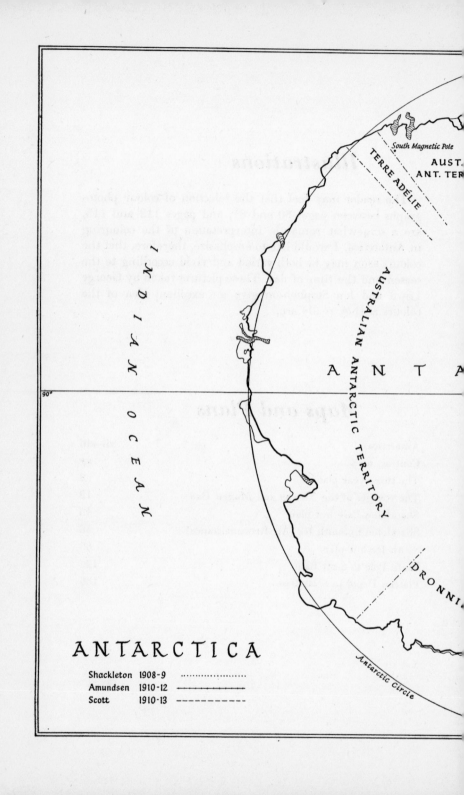

South Magnetic Pole

TERRE ADÉLIE

AUST.
ANT. TER

AUSTRALIAN ANTARCTIC TERRITORY

I N D I A N

O C E A N

90°

A N T A

DRONNI

Antarctic Circle

ANTARCTICA

Shackleton 1908-9   ....
Amundsen   1910-12 —·—·—·—·—
Scott   1910-13 — — — — —

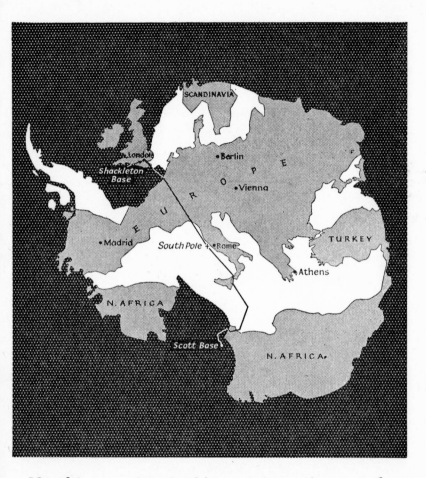

Map of Europe and North Africa superimposed on map of
Antarctica, showing comparative distances.

1. How it all began

The Antarctic is a continent of great size—equal almost to Europe and Australia put together—yet it has no permanent inhabitants. Only those who man weather stations, and the bases from which parties of explorers set out, live there. Some go only for one year, many for two, but never longer, unless the ship which is to bring them out cannot reach their base. In that event they must make the best of it and settle down to another year's work.

Of all this vast continent only about one per cent is exposed rock; all the rest is covered with a mantle of snow and ice, which varies from a few feet to as much as two miles in depth. In all there are over 5,000,000 square miles covered with ice, and this huge area has a tremendous cooling effect on the air which moves over it. It is true to say that the Antarctic controls the weather of the southern half of the world.

Around this dome-shaped continent, which is generally between six and nine thousand feet above sea level, two and three times higher than Snowdon or Ben Nevis, with mountain peaks rising up even higher, lies the great Southern Ocean, formed from the southern parts of the Atlantic, Pacific and Indian Oceans. Together the Antarctic Continent and the Southern Ocean form an area which is almost a fifth of the world's surface. Small wonder then that more and more scientists are visiting the region to acquire new knowledge which will help our better understanding of the earth as a whole.

All round the Antarctic the sea freezes during the winter months of April to October, making it impossible for ships to reach the coast. But in the summer most of this ice breaks up and begins to move with the winds and currents as great fields of ice floes.

Along the coast in the northern parts of the continent the temperature may rise a few degrees above freezing point in the summer, but in winter everything is perpetually frozen. On the coasts south of latitude 75°S it is most unusual for the temperature to rise above freezing point, even in the summer, and during the two years that we were to be at the head of the Weddell Sea this only happened on one day.

As one travels inland and gradually climbs to higher levels, it becomes colder and colder. In 1958 the lowest temperature known in the world was recorded by a Russian party living some hundreds of miles inland from the coast. It was — 124°F, which is 156 degrees of frost!

The sun disappears daily in winter for a longer and longer time the nearer one gets to the Pole. Just south of the Antarctic Circle there is one day in the winter when the sun never rises above the horizon, and at the same point in the summer there will be one day when it never sets. These periods increase as one travels south, until, at the Pole itself, the year is divided into a six-month night and a six-month day.

But the long night is not perpetually dark because during the autumn the rays of the sun are reflected in the sky long after it has sunk below the horizon, and again before it actually reappears in the spring. There is also the moon which comes each month to light the sky. Even this weak light is reflected from the white snow surface, making the whole scene much brighter than in other regions, and during this period (unless the sky is overcast) it is fairly easy to find one's way about.

Imagine then this vast and desolate white continent, fringed here and there with dark rocky mountain ranges. In summer the sun circles the sky and although it is always cold by normal standards, the men who live there find it warm and exhilarating in comparison with the dark winter night, when they cannot travel very far and winds up to a hundred or even two hundred miles an hour blow across the surface, tearing up the snow and driving it in billowing streams that seem to blot out the whole world. Then they cannot move about unless they are heavily clothed and there is the constant risk of frostbite, when fingers, toes or even limbs freeze, the circulation of the blood is destroyed, and men run the risk of amputation when gangrene sets in.

Apart from the journeys of Scott, Amundsen and Shackleton towards the Pole, nothing was known of the interior until recently. All these journeys had started from the Ross Sea side of the continent. In 1908 Shackleton had manhauled his sledges up the Beardmore Glacier and travelled across the polar plateau to within ninety-eight miles of the South Pole itself. Finding himself short of food he then had to turn back to ensure the safety of his party.

Three years later Amundsen and Scott set out from different bases to reach the Pole. Using dog teams, Amundsen was the first to arrive on 14th December 1911. Just over a month later, on 18th January 1912, Scott reached the Pole with four companions, Dr. Wilson, Lieutenant Bowers, Captain Oates and Seaman Evans, only to find there the tent and the Norwegian flag left by Amundsen. They had manhauled their sledges and were exhausted by their terrible journey. On the way back Seaman Evans was injured in a fall and died after considerable suffering; Captain Oates's feet were so badly frostbitten that when he could go no further, he said to his companions, 'I am just going outside and may be some time', and walked out of the tent into the snow to his death, in order not to hold up his friends. Scott, Wilson and Bowers struggled on, but were caught in a blizzard and perished, only eleven miles from the depot which would have saved their lives.

On the Weddell Sea side of the continent only three ships had ever penetrated farther than 70°25′. The first was the *Deutschland* in 1912, carrying the German explorer Filchner. He managed to land on the floating *ice shelf*, but before he could complete his base the ice broke up and his hut floated away. In the end he was forced to abandon his project and sail for home.

In January 1914 Shackleton followed Filchner's route southward on board the *Endurance*, but he was caught in the ice and his ship was finally crushed. The story of how the party lived for over five months in tents on the ice floes and then made their way in small boats to Elephant Island, from where Shackleton

---

An *ice shelf* is a floating sheet of ice of considerable thickness. The seaward cliffs of ice shelves range from six to two hundred feet in height.

sailed to South Georgia to find a rescue ship, is one of the greatest epics of our time.

Both Filchner and Shackleton had planned to cross the continent, but even before he set out Filchner had had to abandon so ambitious an idea owing to lack of money. On the other hand Shackleton started fully equipped, his ships entering both the Weddell and the Ross Seas to set up bases, just as we were to do forty-three years later, but he was defeated by the loss of the *Endurance*.

The third ship to penetrate the area was the Argentine icebreaker *San Martin*, which successfully established the General Belgrano Station at the head of the Weddell Sea in 1954. Though some travelling has been done from this base, it has been confined to the ice shelf around the station.

In the early days of exploration, the famous days of Magellan, Columbus, Raleigh, Cook and Livingstone, the mere fact of discovering a new land, together with the riches that trade might bring, was sufficient reason to launch an expedition. Now, it is scientific facts which men seek in the unknown parts of the world, although the discovery of new mountains is still exciting and, indeed, important.

It was not the crossing of the continent which first gave rise to the planning of the Trans-Antarctic Expedition, but the desire to know more about the geology of the Antarctic; that is, the nature of the rocks which form it and how they came to be built into the mountains which we knew existed. In 1949, when I was working as a geologist for the Falkland Islands Dependencies Survey in the Graham Land Peninsula of the Antarctic, my companion and I, with two dog teams, were four hundred miles from our base, and we were coming to the end of our food. For four days we were confined to our tent by a howling blizzard, only going outside to feed the dogs and to dig up their traces so they could stand up. We lay in our sleeping bags listening to the roaring wind, and our thoughts turned to making plans for a much longer journey—one that would take us right across the huge landmass of the Antarctic, where so much ice is locked up that if it melted, the rise of the sea level would swamp all the ports of the world.

We felt that there was much useful work to be done, for

although in many places round the continent mountains stand proudly clear of the ice, the farther south you go, the more they disappear beneath the all-enveloping dome that is the great ice cap. This is more correctly called the inland ice sheet, for the term 'ice cap' is now used to describe an area smaller than 20,000 square miles, and 'ice sheet' one that is greater. We planned to see what happened to the rocks where they disappeared under the ice—did they continue to form mountains, or was there perhaps a great plateau? Would they lie above or below sea level? Whether, in fact, if all the ice were to be removed, would the Antarctic be revealed as a single huge continent or several large landmasses?

Another study would be to find out whether the whole ice sheet was increasing or decreasing in depth and area, and how the constantly falling snow became incorporated as part of the ice sheet. To aid our seismic work in sounding the ice depth, we would take constant measurements of the strength of gravity. By various calculations these gravity observations could help to determine the thickness of the ice.

No expedition into an unknown land would be complete without a study of the weather, so there would be meteorologists setting up all kinds of instruments to record the sunshine, winds, temperatures, *aurorae* and other phenomena.

Another task which we could usefully do would be to find out as much as possible about our own bodies while they were subjected to a long period of living constantly in very cold conditions. A specially trained doctor would carry out what is known as an 'energy balance'—that is to say, he would measure the amount of food we ate and, by the use of a complex instrument, the amount of oxygen we used up in breathing. The combination of these two produces the energy required by the body for its daily work, and this study would show the amount needed for different tasks under varying conditions of cold.

Aeroplanes and tractors behave differently in extreme cold, so engineers could make a special study of them and find out how the various metals stood the cold and what were the best lubricants to use in these extremes.

It was a fascinating idea, but when I came home in 1950 it took a long time to interest influential people and to raise the £500,000 which such an expedition would cost. However, the Governments of the United Kingdom, New Zealand, Australia and South Africa each provided grants of money, and many hundreds of industrial firms helped us with supplies and equipment. Among our keenest supporters were nearly four thousand schools in the United Kingdom and a great many in New Zealand who 'adopted' the Expedition, raising money for us in all kinds of ingenious ways. One New Zealand school sent £2 10*s*. to our funds made up as follows:

An *aurora* is a luminous phenomenon of the upper atmosphere which appears in the sky as moving streamers or curtains of coloured light. The aurora in the southern skies is known as the *aurora australis*, and in the northern as the *aurora borealis*.

Rabbits' ears	11s.	0d.
Opossum tokens	7s.	6d.
Hedgehog snouts		10½d.
Cash from working at home . .	£1 10s.	0d.

I often wonder where the other 7½d. came from.

In all it was five years before the expedition actually set out. Once we knew that the money would be forthcoming and the different scientific programmes had been worked out in detail, we gave attention to the endless lists of stores and equipment which would be needed, and to making a broad plan of action for what was now called the Commonwealth Trans-Antarctic Expedition.

Normally it is only possible to travel during the light summer months when the temperatures are not so low, therefore our plans for the expedition covered three Antarctic summers, or 'seasons'. In the first year a party would try to penetrate the ice fields of the Weddell Sea and establish a base near Vahsel Bay— the ship remaining there for about three weeks to provide enough men to carry all the stores up to a base site, to build at least the shell of a living hut and to erect the numerous masts and wireless aerials which would help to keep the base in contact with the outside world. An Advance Party of eight men would then be left behind to 'winter'. They would finish building the inside of the hut and begin the scientific programme.

The following year two more parties would go south—the Main or Crossing Party to join those already there, in time to set up a small scientific station about three hundred miles inland which would be manned by three men during the second winter. At the same time a second party, the Ross Sea Party, would sail from New Zealand to the Ross Sea to establish another base in McMurdo Sound on the other side of the continent. New Zealand undertook to establish this base, and Sir Edmund Hillary was appointed leader of the Ross Sea Party. Besides carrying out scientific work, this party would try to find a safe vehicle route up one of the glaciers that lead on to the polar plateau, and would lay out depots of food and fuel towards the South Pole.

In the third season the Crossing Party would attempt to cross the continent from the Weddell Sea to the Ross Sea, using the

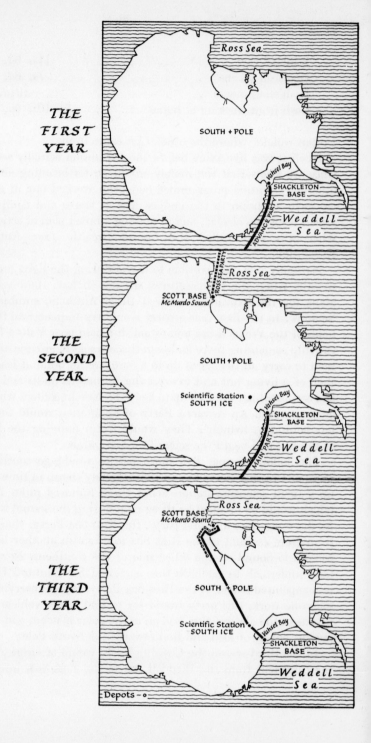

THE COMMONWEALTH TRANS–ANTARCTIC EXPEDITION
The Three-Year Plan

THE FIRST YEAR

Ross Sea

SOUTH + POLE

Vahsel Bay
SHACKLETON BASE
ADVANCE PARTY
Weddell Sea

THE SECOND YEAR

ROSS PARTY
Ross Sea

SCOTT BASE
McMurdo Sound

SOUTH + POLE

Scientific Station
SOUTH ICE

Vahsel Bay
SHACKLETON BASE
MAIN PARTY
Weddell Sea

THE THIRD YEAR

SCOTT BASE
McMurdo Sound
Ross Sea

SOUTH + POLE

Scientific Station
SOUTH ICE

Vahsel Bay
SHACKLETON BASE

Weddell Sea

Depots – o

inland station as their final food and fuel depot before setting out for the Pole. Beyond this they would pick up the depots established by the Ross Sea Party from McMurdo Sound.

Both parties would use mechanical transport, with dog teams and aircraft for reconnaissance.

We decided to attempt the crossing with four Sno-Cat tractors and four Weasels, while two small Ferguson tractors and a Bombardier Muskeg from Canada would be used for work around the Weddell Sea base site. The Sno-Cats came from America—weighing three tons, they had 200 h.p. engines and four independent tracks each eight feet long. Each 'cat' could carry one ton of stores and equipment and tow five to six tons behind on two sledges. The maximum speed with this load was 10 m.p.h., though we were seldom to attain this.

The Weasels were smaller, with only two tracks, and carried a load of half a ton with two and a half to three tons on one sledge. Both vehicles used about the same amount of petrol, covering 0·8 to 1·25 miles per gallon.

The little Fergusons were ordinary farm tractors fitted with tracks over the wheels. These were intended only for use at the bases but, as you shall read, they were actually driven as far as the South Pole.

Over a thousand men (and several women too) applied to join the expedition and from these, nineteen were chosen for the party going to the Weddell Sea and twenty-three to go to the Ross Sea.

Our clothing would consist of heavy mesh string vests over which we would wear woollen vests, shirts and sweaters. Trousers would be the normal Army battledress type worn over long wollen pants. Out of doors those of us doing active work or ski-ing all day with dog teams would wear anoraks and trousers made of windproof material which would prevent the layer of warm air round our bodies from being blown away by the wind. The windproofs to be issued to the tractor drivers, who would be sitting still in the bitter cold most of the day, would be lined with nylon fur.

Various kinds of boots were ordered for different types of work and temperature. Inside these the men could wear several pairs of socks and a number of soft felt slippers known as duffels. Our hands would be protected by fingerless leather gauntlets inside which we could wear thick felt hand duffels and woollen gloves. Each man would also have an assortment of woollen caps, windproof hoods and protective 'blizzard masks' from which he could choose his headgear according to the weather conditions.

Planning the stores was an enormous task. The sledging ration for men and dogs would consist mainly of pemmican, butter and biscuits. Pemmican is a mixture of beef extract and fat, but as it does not taste very nice by itself it is usually disguised with some curry powder. All the food would be made up to give the right proportions to maintain health, and compressed to take up as little space as possible.

At base we would live on a normal diet and among the items which were eventually taken were 6,973 tins of vegetables (including 115 5-lb. tins of dehydrated cabbage) and 69 Christmas puddings!

In addition, all the scientific equipment had to be designed, bought, tested, adjusted and, if necessary, modified. Hundreds of engineering tools and spare parts were to be assembled, while the vehicles would go through many factories where specialized work could be done on them before they were placed in 'cold chambers', where the temperature was reduced to −60°F to make sure that all the parts worked properly in these conditions.

It was a busy time for everyone, for while preparing and assembling the 350 tons of stores to go south in the first ship, we had also to make the final detailed plans for the expedition itself. It must be remembered that when exploring one must be able to adjust plans to meet the unexpected conditions and events which occur. We knew, even before we left England, that we could not expect everything to happen exactly as planned, but we were happy in the knowledge that we were equipped to deal with most of the difficulties which might arise. The challenge of exploratory work is to overcome the difficult problems set by nature, and now we looked forward with the greatest keenness and excitement to the tasks we had set ourselves and the challenge we had accepted.

2. The voyage of the Theron

On 14th November 1955 nineteen of us left the Pool of London in the white-painted *Theron* to the cheerful tooting of the tugs and river steamers and the shouted good wishes of the small crowds gathered on the wharves and jetties all the way down to Gravesend. With us came Ed Hillary, his second-in-command 'Bob' Miller, and his senior pilot, Squadron-Leader John Claydon of the R.N.Z.A.F.; the three of them were on board to gain experience of Antarctic conditions before going back to New Zealand to organize their own team.

The Advance Party which was to 'winter' south would be led by Kenneth Blaiklock, a slight fair-haired young surveyor who had already spent four years in the Antarctic. The deputy leader was Ralph Lenton, with five winters to his credit, who was to be in charge of hut construction; but his ability to turn his hand to anything was a great asset. He proved to be the best cook among us and an enthusiastic radio 'ham' operator. During the second winter south, he contacted fifty-six different countries and made radio friends all over the world.

The most important part of our scientific work during the first year concerned the weather, and so there were three meteorologists: Tony Stewart, a master at the Nautical College, Pangbourne; Peter Jeffries, lent to us by the Air Ministry, and 'Hannes' La Grange, a South African who came from the Weather Bureau in Pretoria. Beside being a splendid worker, Hannes never seemed to stop talking, especially on the radio, and before long the expression 'maundering' was in frequent use to describe anyone who was apt to babble on. Endless radio chats with other bases were to become known as 'having a maunder'.

The wintering party was completed by Dr. Rainer Goldsmith,

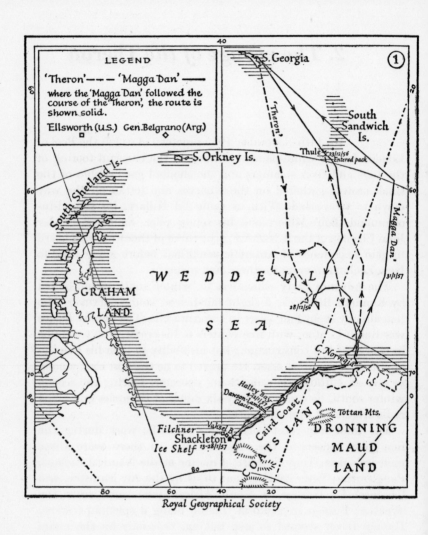

LEGEND

'Theron' ----- 'Magga Dan' ———

where the 'Magga Dan' followed the course of the 'Theron', the route is shown solid.

Ellsworth (U.S.) □ Gen. Belgrano (Arg.) ◇

S. Georgia

South Sandwich Is.

Thule × 23/12/56
Entered pack

'Theron'

'Magga Dan'

31/1/57

S. Orkney Is.

South Shetland Is.

W E D D E L L

S E A

GRAHAM LAND

28/12/56

C. Norvegia

Halley Bay 4-31/1/57
Dawson-Lambton Glacier

Vahsel B.

Filchner
Shackleton
Ice Shelf 13-28/1/57

COATS LAND

CAIRD COAST

Töttan Mts.

DRONNING MAUD LAND

Royal Geographical Society

①

nicknamed 'Rhino', Sergeant-Major 'Roy' Homard from R.E.M.E., our second engineer, and Sergeant Ellis Williams, a radio operator, lent by the R.A.F., who, being a Welshman, was always known as 'Taffy'. Short and quite imperturbable, Taffy was never without a cigarette, but at regular intervals throughout the expedition he would decide to give up smoking, and would lay bets all round that he could succeed. For several days he would keep his good resolution, and then, if one entered the radio-room unexpectedly, there was a tell-tale whiff and a guilty look on Taffy's face—although he steadfastly denied everything! Gradually he would relapse into smoking in public again. He once took the drastic step of deliberately going on a three-week journey without any tobacco, but as the days passed and none of his companions was a smoker, he became more and more desperate, and was finally bribing the pilots with sweets to bring him out a packet of cigarettes from base, offering to swap his chocolate ration for months ahead!

The *Theron*, commanded by Captain Harald Marø, was a Canadian sealer of 859 tons. Her holds were bulging with our stores and every inch of deck space contained the overflow. At one end was a huge crate holding our Sno-Cat tractor—at the other, the little single-engined Auster aircraft to be used for reconnaissance once we entered the ice. In between, the whole deck was covered with hundreds of fuel barrels, and on top of these were stowed the stove pipes for our Aga cooker, oxygen cylinders for the engineering workshop, a dinghy, a spare Auster, dozens of assorted packing cases which would not fit into the holds and twenty-four slatted crates containing the huskies which had come from Greenland. As we crossed the Equator two families were born and suddenly we had fourteen puppies to look after and exercise. To accommodate them 'play-pens' were built round each mother's kennel, but to get from one end of the ship to the other we had to clamber over all this assortment, and when it was rough it was quite an exciting adventure.

Contrary to popular imagination, huskies are very affectionate dogs and are only dangerous to man if they have been ill-treated. Perhaps their reputation comes from their eagerness to fight among themselves, which they will do at the slightest provocation. About the same size as an Alsatian, they love working as a team, and for their own driver will work almost till they drop, but a stranger is lucky if he can even get them to start. Immensely strong, their thick, oily coat helps them to survive incredibly severe conditions and still haul heavy loads on only one pound of food a day. Of course, they must usually have more, but for a journey of a month or two they will work hard and keep healthy on as little as this.

By the middle of December we reached Grytviken in South Georgia and here we fitted wings to the Auster, which was then test-flown. The day we left, a few tall icebergs were seen, the largest standing 250 feet above the water and quite unaffected by the swell which was making the ship plunge heavily and drove many of our party to their bunks. On 21st December we were recording the first temperature below freezing point and throughout the ship there was an air of expectancy—everyone was waiting for the ice! Captain Marø because he loved to work his ship through it, some of us because of the feeling that at last we were getting to grips with our first problem, and many because of the relief it would bring from rolling and pitching.

Just before Christmas Day we entered a belt of loose ice made up of *brash*, *growlers* and *bergy bits*, scattered over the water as far as the eye could see. In the next few days the ice gradually thickened and sometimes a huge piece would become wedged beneath the bow of the ship, extending perhaps twelve or fifteen feet down into the water, slowing our speed and upsetting the steering. From time to time we killed seals to provide food for our dogs and to build up a reserve for the coming winter, and as we entered the pack we met our first penguins. The large Emperors were stately, dignified and quite disinterested in our doings, but the cheeky little Adélies hastened over to satisfy their curiosity about our every move.

Ice floes are free pieces of sea ice, large or small. Ice up to three feet thick forms 'light floes', thicker floes are called 'heavy floes'. Floes may be ten miles or more in diameter. *Brash* consists of small fragments of broken ice not larger than six feet across; it is the wreckage of other forms of ice. *Growlers* are pieces of ice almost awash, smaller than *bergy bits*, which are massive pieces of ice generally less than fifteen feet above sea level and not more than thirty feet across.

David Pratt, our senior engineer, was tall, wavy haired and very energetic. Never having seen an Adélie before, he determined to catch one. To his surprise he found it far too nimble as it skated round and round an ice hummock, with him in close pursuit. Quickly it learned to climb up a soft snow slope, pause at the top for David to flounder after it, and then, just as he reached out to grab it, scoot down the far side on its stomach. Unable to copy this, David fell flat on his face time after time, much to the delight of another Adélie who had joined us in admiring his gymnastic display.

On Boxing Day our troubles began. The open *leads* and pools of water through which we had been passing ended and we reached an area of large old *hummocked ice* through which it became increasingly difficult to penetrate, until at midday we found ourselves jammed between enormous floes and cemented by a mush of broken fragments and slushy snow which held the ship in a vice-like grip.

It took four hours to break free and from then onwards our progress was slow and tortuous as the ice situation constantly changed under the effect of winds and current, and the narrow leads closed with the pressure of the floes. All the time the *Theron* remained heading south, although we had determined that the only thing to do was to extricate ourselves northward to the open sea, and then re-enter the pack on a different course. But the ice was so close that we could not find a place where there was sufficient water to turn her.

Day after day, time after time, for hours on end, everyone was over the side with axes, shovels, boards and boat hooks, clearing ice from the ship. Some of us would hack at the huge piled-up floes and prise them free with crowbars, while others poled the loosened pieces back into the wash of the propeller. Sometimes we fired explosives to dislodge the *Theron* from a position in which she had become perched, unable to move either forwards or backwards.

By the end of December we were beset, held unable to move in the ice, and drifting fifteen to twenty miles each day with the huge ice field that kept us prisoner. Then for three weeks it was overcast, and not being able to see the sun we could not fix our position accurately, but we remained so long in the same place that we even gave the icebergs names. The little ship struggled gamely to force a passage through. Time after time, with a resounding crash, she charged forward. Everything creaked and groaned, and then the bows rose high in the air as she climbed the floe. Always we hoped that her weight would break a passage through and enable us to move a few yards, but usually the ice was too thick, and the *Theron* slid backwards into the small pool

---

A *lead* is a navigable passage of water through pack ice.
Hummocked ice is sea ice piled haphazardly one piece over another, which may be weathered or mantled with snow.

which contained her in the middle of the endless expanse of the ice field.

I wrote in my journal:

> It is impossible to describe adequately this forceful butting of the ice. The ship runs up through crowded brash, forcing three- or four-foot plates of ice beneath the keel, or up-ending them alongside the hull. Then, with a shuddering bump, the bows rise on a floe—up and up we seem to go—when suddenly she subsides and cracks go shooting across the ice. At other times she hangs there with her bows up and we go astern to try once more. Over and over again the process is repeated, gradually breaking away the obstruction, while the ship twists and shudders till one feels she will fall apart. The most frightening noises are when the propeller strikes the ice and a thundering hammering shakes us from stem to stern, or when going astern the rudder butts a heavy floe and the hydraulic release valve screeches in apparent agony.

Unless we could soon find a way into open water it would be too late in the season to establish a base this first year, and the Trans-Antarctic Expedition would have failed before it had even begun. It was a very anxious time.

Meanwhile the daily chores kept us all busy. The supply of fresh water was getting low so an ingenious cauldron was rigged on the after deck and each day we chipped a ton of ice from the surrounding hummocks, formed a human chain and passed the blocks along to the ship to be melted for our needs. Although this was sea ice, it was old enough for the salt to have been excluded by the freezing, so that the water was clear and sweet.

If only we could have flown the plane, the pilot might have been able to see a path which would take us into open water, but although the Auster could operate either on floats or skis, we could find neither a pool of water nor a smooth enough air strip between all the hummocked ice floes which surrounded us.

As well as John Claydon of the New Zealand party, we had two other pilots on board: Squadron-Leader John Lewis and Flight-Lieutenant Gordon Haslop of the R.A.F. John Lewis was a large rotund man, full of high spirits and with a great sense of the ridiculous. When being measured for his polar clothing, he had discovered his true shape. He grinned: 'I'm 42–44–46. Call me Pear.'

Gordon Haslop was a cheerful New Zealander with a wide experience of flying many different types of aircraft in out of the way places, and we soon learned to have great confidence in his judgement, for, in the course of the expedition, everything happened to Gordon.

Another New Zealander in our party was George Lowe, the official photographer. Tall and lanky, double-jointed nearly everywhere, he could take up the most astonishing and absurd postures at unexpected moments, and he and Gordon singing Maori songs in parts were a favourite double-act at our festivities.

Flight-Sergeant Peter Weston of the R.A.F. came to look after our aircraft and was responsible for keeping them operational, and our numbers were completed by my second-in-command, David Stratton, who was a surveyor and also acted as our very hard-working stores officer.

During the third week in January the wind suddenly changed and the current at last carried us to within sight of a small pool about three hundred and fifty yards long with a dog-leg in the middle—just, but only just, long enough for the Auster to take off. At last there was a chance to fly! We renewed our efforts to break through the intervening ice floes, and when, after some hours, we succeeded, the Auster was quickly lowered over the side.

It was John Claydon's turn to fly, and, as he motored round and round warming up the engine, the bridge and chart-room hummed with activity. John Lewis was flying controller and had the use of radio, Aldis lamp, different coloured Very lights, smoke candles and other 'fireworks'. The radio-room stood by, with Ralph Lenton and Taffy Williams working the equipment, which included a radio beacon. In the chart-room Gordon Haslop was 'plotter', ready to record the position of the aircraft, while David Stratton and Ken Blaiklock would plot the ice reports on special map sheets as they were received from the pilot.

John had told us over the radio that he would make a dummy run first, so that he could find out how the plane would behave on the curving take-off. We watched anxiously from the ship as the aircraft took the dog-leg and the wash from its floats curved out across the still water. Then, suddenly, we realized that this was no dummy run; nearer and nearer John approached the ice at the end of the pool; it seemed impossible that he could clear it and the airmen among us hardly dared to look—but, at the very last moment, only a few feet away from the edge, the plane lifted and was airborne. A three-hour reconnaissance flight had begun.

When John returned we asked him why he had so suddenly decided to take off. 'I had to make it on the first run,' he said. 'I would never have dared to have another go!' His flight established that we were about fifty miles from the open sea to the north and John was able to advise Captain Marø what course to steer to bring us clear. In the nick of time we had found a way out.

During the last week that we were beset, a Royal Naval patrol vessel, H.M.S. *Protector*, was operating in the Falkland Islands Dependencies, over a thousand miles away, and kindly offered to come to our help. She carried helicopters which could reconnoitre the area for us, and was now steaming towards the ice edge. Her daily signals reporting progress always ended: 'Speed 12 knots.' That evening I sent back a message of thanks explaining, rather apologetically, that we now seemed to have found a way out. This merely spurred Captain Wilkinson to greater efforts and we received a reply stating firmly, 'Am now proceeding to your assistance at 17 knots!'

On 23rd January the *Protector* reached the ice edge to the north of us, and her helicopter found us steaming through narrow leads at six knots. Everyone in the helicopter and nearly everyone in the ship had cameras trained on the other, and later, when we met the ship just outside the pack ice, many of us went on board for dinner. The whaler sent to bring us over was bobbing about like a cork as we clambered twenty feet up a swaying rope ladder to reach the quarterdeck. A kindly sailor, showing great concern for Ed Hillary's safety, was heard to say: 'Hold tight, sir —think you can make it?'

To which a scornful coxswain replied: 'Of course he can make it—climbed Everest didn't he?'

Now we again began our assault on the Antarctic Continent, setting course for Cape Norvegia in Dronning Maud Land, where

19

we hoped to make our landfall. We believed that in the summer a lead of open water formed along the coast and we hoped to be able to follow this for a long distance southwards—perhaps even to the head of the Weddell Sea itself.

At this time many countries were establishing bases in the Antarctic in preparation for the International Geophysical Year which would begin in June 1957. This was to be a period during which many different observations would be made at the same time from numerous scientific stations all over the world. In the almost deserted Antarctic, it was necessary to build a number of new stations to do this work so that there would not be a gap in the network of observations which were planned to envelop the earth. Great Britain's contribution to the I.G.Y. was an expedition sent by the Royal Society in an even smaller ship than ours called the *Tottan*, which had left England a week after the *Theron*. Avoiding the difficulties we had encountered, she had reached 75°36′S, 26°45′W, three weeks ahead of us, and here the Expedition had begun to set up their base. The Royal Society decided to name the bay where the *Tottan* was now unloading, Halley Bay, as a tribute to the memory of the famous astronomer Edmund Halley, who was born in 1656.

On 27th January we arrived at this point, sailing along a magnificent cliff coastline in perfect sunny weather. In our imagination it seemed like the white cliffs of Dover, the sandy beach bleached by a perpetual sun, the holidaymakers represented by basking seals and groups of penguins. Two small black figures were waving from the ice edge as we approached, and we recognized David Dalgliesh, the leader of the Royal Society Expedition, and George Lush, who had come down to meet and guide us to the base site two miles inland, where their party were building a living hut. A boat was lowered to bring them on board, and soon ice anchors were put out. As greetings were being exchanged, the Auster was put over the side, while a second party prepared to go sealing and yet others set about the usual collection of ice for our water supply.

Halley Bay was not a suitable point for us to build our base because the area behind was heavily crevassed and there was no possible vehicle route to the south, so after twenty-four hours we said goodbye and continued sailing along the coast for another two hundred miles, always searching for a base site at a point where we could conveniently unload the ship and also travel inland towards the Pole.

Most of the time the *land-water* lead we were following was about three miles wide, with the high cliffs of the ice shelf on one side, and a maze of interlocking ice floes, much too thick for the *Theron* to break through, on the other. At one point it narrowed to only a hundred yards for many miles, and our experienced Captain knew that it would be dangerous to sail along it. Yet, in his determination that the expedition should reach its destination, he steamed on. Had the wind and current, which had forced the ice apart, allowed it to close again around us, it was unlikely that even the stout build of the *Theron* could have withstood its pressure. She would certainly have been locked in for the winter, and would probably have been crushed.

Gordon Haslop flew me ahead of the ship, looking for a site. Finally we reached Vahsel Bay—as far south as a ship can go—and then chose a point on the sea ice twenty-eight miles to the west, where the *Theron* could be unloaded. There she was moored, about half a mile from the fairly steep slope which led up to the top of the ice shelf itself. The hut would be built a further mile inland.

We had decided to call our base after Sir Ernest Shackleton, whose original plans for a trans-Antarctic journey had failed in 1914. After years of planning and months of preparation we had at last reached the exact spot pinpointed on the map in our London office long before, and on the evening of 29th January 1956 we sent a telegram to our headquarters reporting that Shackleton Post Office had been opened. Later we were to find that the base was 195 feet above sea level, that the ice beneath was 1,300 feet thick and was floating on 3,000 feet of water.

So ended the outward voyage of the *Theron*. Our next task was to unload the stores and start building the hut as quickly as possible, for already the weather was getting worse, temperatures were falling, and none of us knew how long the ship would be able to remain.

Land-water is an area of open sea water forming each year along a coast when the sea ice is forced away from the shore by the wind. Its proper name is a *shore lead*.

3. Shackleton Base

There was no time to waste, and as the ice anchors went out, several of us set off to find a suitable site for the base. Once this was done, unloading began in a frenzy of activity; this being a period of continuous daylight it was possible to work at any time and we instituted a sixteen-hour working day. First off the ship were the dogs and we were all happy to watch their wild excitement—overjoyed to be on firm ice again, they ate, dug and

rolled in the snow, howling their pleasure. Soon they were all
picketed, each attached by a ten-foot chain at regular intervals to
long steel cables laid out on the snow. Throughout the long voyage we had washed out the kennels daily and done all we could
to make their conditions bearable, but the confined space, the heat
of the Tropics and the constant rolling of the ship was inevitably
distressing for animals used only to the snows of Greenland. We
were proud to find that our efforts had helped them to come
through the experience in fine condition.

Next the large Sno-Cat crate was slung over the side, followed
by the deck cargo of fuel drums, and soon the forward hold was
open and stores were pouring out—two Weasels, two Ferguson
tractors, sledges, hut timbers, generators, ration boxes, tools,
medical stores, scientific equipment, coal—in all we had over
350 tons to handle in a race against time.

Our first task was to test the route to the top of the ice shelf,
which David Stratton and I had already marked with flags, and

to make safe the open cracks along the edges of some wide
crevasses lying between the ship and the Shackleton base site. For
this six of us set off with a tractor towing two sledges. On one was
an eleven-hundredweight diesel generator; on the other, timber,
tools and marker flags. All went well crossing the half-mile of sea
ice, but as soon as we began the steep climb up the drifted slope
of the ice shelf where the snow was soft, the sledge runners sank
deeply and the tractor began to dig itself in. Finally we had to
leave the generator at the foot of the slope, taking on only one
sledge. It was clear that we would not be able to haul full loads up
the slope to the top of the ice shelf, and we realized that the task
would take almost twice as long as we had expected. We therefore decided to make a stores depot at the top of the ice shelf, thus
saving two miles of driving for every load. To do this we began
marking out various circuits for the vehicles and marking the
sites for the stores dumps with poles and flags. On the very first
circuit a tractor broke through into two concealed crevasses running at right angles to those which we could see, and showing that
the apparently innocent area was far from safe. Although a
vehicle would probably not drop through these narrow crevasses,
men on foot certainly could not move about safely in such a
place. The only alternative was to form the depot on the sea ice
at the foot of the slope. This we now did, although some stores
continued to reach the base site hauled by the Weasel, which was
the only vehicle able to haul full loads up the slope.

During the first night the R.A.F. contingent replaced the
Auster's floats with skis so that the plane could be put over the
side of the *Theron* out of the way of unloading operations. Once it
was on the sea ice John Lewis started the engine and, with
Gordon Haslop and Peter Weston clinging to the wings to balance
her, the plane was motored away to previously prepared pickets
on a smooth stretch of ice about three hundred yards from the
ship. From then on, whenever the weather was suitable, we made
reconnaissance flights inland to discover some of the problems
which would face us when we started on our journey during the
next season.

On the morning of 1st February work began under an over-

A *crevasse* is a deep open crack, or fissure, in the surface of the ice.

cast sky. One of the Weasels developed a fault and the spare part required was deep in No. 2 hold, which had not yet been opened. Unloading had been kept down to a rate which allowed all the stores to be removed immediately to the safety of the dumps, for no matter how solid sea ice may appear to be, it is not wise to stack material directly beside the ship. I had to decide whether to leave the Weasel out of use, which meant that we had only the second Weasel to move material up to the top of the ice shelf itself (for our Ferguson tractors could not haul the heavy loads up the soft slope), or to take the risk of unloading more quickly and stacking stores beside the ship. Because we were so short of time I decided to open up No. 2 hold at once and mend the second Weasel.

No sooner had we accumulated a considerable pile of equipment on the sea ice than the wind rose and heavy squalls of snow began driving over us from the north. By the afternoon a real blizzard was blowing, the roaring wind bringing a drift so thick that it was necessary to put out markers every fifty yards for the tractor drivers to find their way to the foot of the ice shelf. Soon the sea began to rise and waves slapped angrily against the ice edge, bursting over and flooding the surface, until a snowy quagmire formed around the piles of stores stacked near the ship. The *Theron* herself was grinding against the ice, her plates groaning in protest, and straining heavily on her after mooring cables. As more and more water poured over the ice edge and flooded the stores area, we worked frantically to salvage all we could before the cases became saturated with salt water, the tractors hauling the loaded sledges inland through the blinding snow as fast as they could.

Five men were working up at Shackleton and I sent a message telling them to return to the ship immediately as it was obvious that Captain Marø would probably have to move her from the ice edge if the *pack ice* began closing in from the north. Within an hour or two the water was two feet deep over a wide area, and our dinghy was being used to salvage floating cases. Everyone had become so wet that there was no longer any point in avoiding

---

Pack ice is any area of sea ice other than *fast ice*, which is unbroken sea ice, varying in width, and remaining attached to the coast.

wading in the slush and water. The tractors were still hauling away stores as fast as possible, but in spite of all our efforts the battle was partly lost, for many boxes were floating and some were completely submerged. We dared not think what they might contain. Tinned foods would remain undamaged, but with some dismay I found myself standing on two submerged cases marked: B.B.C. RECORDING EQUIPMENT—HANDLE WITH CARE!

At this moment I saw the *Theron*'s stern cables part and the ship began to swing slowly away from the ice edge. Immediately I shouted to the members of the crew who were working with us to run for the ship and try to scramble aboard before a gap opened between the bows and the ice. Splashing their way through the water, they floundered across the hundred yards to the ship and just managed to clamber aboard with the aid of ropes and ladders hastily thrown over the side. Relieved to know that at least Captain Marø had a complete crew, the rest of us arrived in time to see the ship swing completely round, part her bow cables and slowly drift away from us. As the driving snow and drift blotted her from our sight the Captain was shouting through a megaphone from a wing of the bridge and we could just make out his words, 'We'll be ba-a-ck'—a long, drawn-out call that carried above the howling wind.

The men up at base still had not returned, but there was now a more immediate problem, for twelve of us were on the ice with soaking feet and legs, and we did not know how long it would take for the ship to turn round and come back—indeed it might not even be possible for her to come back to the same landing place, for as we continued salvaging our stores, huge crumpled masses of *pressure ice* could be seen lurching past with the wind and current, turning and heaving with the waves as they rolled their way along past the ice edge. Fortunately the temperature was 26°F, only six degrees below freezing point, but had it dropped much lower we should indeed have been in trouble. While my mind revolved about the problem of shelter and the whereabouts of spare clothing in the hundreds of cases now stacked ashore, we kept reasonably warm by hauling sledges,

---

Pressure ice is a general term for sea ice which has been squeezed, and in places forced upwards, when it can be described as 'rafted ice', 'hummocked ice', or 'pressure ridge'.

digging out bogged down tractors and heaving packing cases from the ever deepening sludge of snow and water.

After half an hour a shout drew my attention seaward—and I saw the *Theron* suddenly looming mysteriously and silently through the driving blizzard. First her bows and foremast, then the whole ship gradually emerged like a wraith from the tearing white wall that enveloped everything, and we could hear Captain Marø urging us to hurry and shouting, 'You'll have to jump aboard while she's moving.'

Carefully judging his time, the Captain nosed his vessel in to the ice edge between two huge drifting masses, bringing her close alongside the old landing site. Over the side were hanging every rope and rope-ladder that the crew could muster, and as the ship slid past we leapt across the narrow gap of surging water, grabbed them and scrambled our way up the sides.

One rope thrown from the bows to the ice was seized by Gordon Haslop. As he began to climb, it swung vertically from the overhanging bows, and poor Gordon found himself suspended over the swirling water, quite unable to negotiate the overhang above. Luckily two of us were able to rescue him from his predicament by grasping the end before it fell into the water and hauling his dangling legs back on to solid ice!

Roy Homard also found himself in trouble. Scrambling up the side of the ship he ended up standing on the bulwarks with the sheer side of an aircraft crate towering above him. There he remained, unable to move in any direction, with the ship moving away from the ice edge, until some of us could reach down to him from the top of the crate and pull him to safety.

We now had on board the full crew and fourteen members of the expedition—leaving David Stratton, Ralph Lenton, David Pratt, Bob Miller and Peter Jeffries ashore still facing the storm. As Captain Marø moved into open water the drift was so thick that he could only navigate by radar. As the ship broke through a narrow stretch of heavy floes we were relieved to feel her rise to a gentle swell, for this meant that there must be extensive open water to the north. All through the night we either drifted or went half-ahead to keep clear of the coastal ice where more and more floes were gathering until two miles of pack ice lay between us and our landing site.

27

The next day the northerly wind continued until three in the afternoon, but by four o'clock it suddenly began to blow from the south and we were able to nose our way in towards the ice edge through a steady snowfall. Miraculously, it seemed, the great accumulation of pack ice moved slowly away, and Captain Marø was able to bring the ship right back to the original mooring place. As we approached, what a relief it was to see figures moving about among the tethered dogs and the piles of stores! As we came within hailing distance Bob Miller found a standing camera tripod we had abandoned in our rush and we could see him cranking an imaginary camera at the ship, while David Stratton, who had been firing red recognition signals, held his stomach and yelled, 'Guess what we had for breakfast?'

Soon they were all on board changing into dry clothes and we heard the story of their ordeal. On getting my message the party had tried to get back to the ship, but even with the aid of stakes we had driven into the ice along the route, they had lost their way in the driving drift even before reaching the edge of the ice shelf, so had very sensibly settled down to await clearer conditions. It is difficult enough for five people to arrange themselves in a Weasel already holding a wireless set and other gear, let alone try to sleep for several hours in freezing conditions. From time to time the heater was turned on, but this made them too hot—and they became bitterly cold again as soon as it was turned off. Every half hour the vehicle was moved forward a yard or two so that the big sledge behind it would not become drifted up. After four hours the weather conditions improved sufficiently for them to find their way down on to the sea ice—and then they knew for the first time that the *Theron* had gone, and that they were on their own for an indefinite time.

For two or three hours they continued the salvage work which had been abandoned when the rest of us had scrambled aboard the ship, and then they returned to the base site and crowded into a small 'caboose', a tea-break shelter, which had been made from some packing cases the day before. They found this very cramped quarters for five men, and by the time they had rolled themselves in bulky strips of Fibreglass to try and keep warm, they seemed almost to be lying on top of one another. By three in the morning the cold and restless night no longer seemed bearable, so a hot drink of sugar and milk-powder was brewed and for breakfast they made a hotchpotch of sardines, tomatoes and sugar, all stirred together in one tin.

Feeling much better after this feast, and finding that the wind had dropped considerably, they pitched three tents for use in any future emergency, and then went down to the sea ice again to continue salvaging the stores. It was then ten in the morning—imagine their relief when seven hours later they caught sight of the *Theron* as she emerged from the curtain of falling snow and moved slowly in to the old landing site.

With the ship once more safely moored, we set to work in the snowy morass to recover the remainder of our equipment, which was already beginning to freeze into a solid mass. Everything had to be towed some distance to dry snow before it could be loaded on to a sledge. Not only were the cases full of salt water, but thick layers of snow sludge stuck to the outside of each, adding greatly to the weight. It was back-breaking work.

During the next few days unloading continued apace. The thermometer fell to 2°F, and owing to the difference in temperature between air and water (for the sea was relatively warm), 'frost-smoke' rose like steam and drifted away in the wind. It was fascinating to watch, for the sea looked like the surface of a gigantic boiling cauldron.

By 5th February it was getting steadily colder, weather conditions were getting worse and the shore lead was narrowing. We realized that the ship might have to leave at an hour's notice. Half the hutting and twenty-five tons of coal still remained in the holds and the tempo of our work increased, while the members of the Advance Party packed all their belongings, ready for an immediate landing.

As the tractors moved to and from the ship, the drivers could be recognized by the way they perched on the bouncing metal seats. On at least one occasion we saw George Lowe driving with his legs lying along the bonnet of the Ferguson, while in his remarkable, double-jointed way he managed to recline on the bouncing seat in a carefree manner. Singing happily, he disappeared into the distance, the tractor and sledge apparently looking after themselves.

On 6th February we had completed unloading, and stores once

more began to go up to the Shackleton site. There Ralph Lenton started reconstructing the Sno-Cat crate, which was intended to serve as an emergency shelter for the building party and later as a workshop. We little thought then that eight men would have to live in it right through the long polar night.

That evening John Lewis and I flew inland in the Auster. At thirty miles from Vahsel Bay, when we were at 6,000 feet, John suddenly said, 'Look! What's that on the horizon?' Gazing through binoculars I could make out a distant ridge-like line of white and dark—certainly a far distant range of mountains lying due south of us. So we experienced the excitement of our first discovery.

We judged them to be several thousand feet high and at least seventy-five miles distant. Our first instinct was to set course for them to find out what sort of barrier they might present to our southern travelling on the ground. But we had already lost radio contact with the ship and our fuel was getting low, so we were forced to turn for home. On our return, as a tribute to the in-domitable *Theron* and her Captain, we decided to call this range the Theron Mountains. The news of our discovery caused excite-ment among our surveyors and geologists who could now look forward to a definite task instead of being faced with the prospect of never-ending, featureless snow fields.

The next day Gordon flew Ken Blaiklock over these mountains while he made a sketch map of the area which would be helpful when he started southward to reconnoitre the first part of our route in the 1956–7 season. On board the *Theron* we anxiously awaited the return of the aircraft, for the wind had changed to the north-east and was now driving the pack ice towards the ship, so that every minute the open lead in which we lay became narrower. As the pack closed in, it compressed and over-rafted the thin skin of ice which had formed during the night. It was fascinating but rather ominous to watch the ice breaking into many-tongued plates, which slid silently one over the other like loose playing cards, rebuilding themselves into a pack. Ever moving, always thickening, buckling, sliding, advancing on the ship, it seemed that the ice was alive, and moving with the silent purpose of our destruction.

At half-past twelve Captain Marø decided that the ship must

leave within an hour, but the Auster was still airborne. As the minutes passed the new ice continued to thicken round us and the pack gradually closed the mile-wide sheet to a width of less than a hundred yards. An hour later, when the plane landed, the sludge and over-rafted ice was already eighteen inches thick around the side of the ship, and away to the east we could see a tongue of pack ice approaching the coast, threatening to close our escape route in that direction.

Haste was now vital or we should be cemented in for the winter. The Advance Party had already stowed their belongings on a sledge, ready to go up to Shackleton—it only remained for us to hoist the plane on board and cast off. We were leaving them with a formidable task—the ship had only been at Shackleton for nine days and all we had been able to do for them was to get the stores ashore. None of us liked to feel that the expedition was dividing into two, and those of us who were going home to prepare the next stage felt that we were somehow leaving our companions in the lurch. Suddenly we were all shaking hands and receiving last-minute notes and messages for families in England, and then the siren hooted and we were back on board, waving and shouting to eight men standing rather forlornly on the ice edge with their dogs, assuring us that they would be all right.

The *Theron* slid slowly away, turning in a wide sweep on to an easterly course, while Gordon fired a farewell Very light on to the ice. Three long blasts of the siren drowned the final shouts and we found ourselves silently waving to the little group, which seemed so quickly to dwindle until we could no longer distinguish individual figures. It would be a year before we were all together again, during which time they were to endure the most lonely and prolonged ordeal of the whole expedition.

The ship pushed forward and the floating ice sludge parted and re-formed again behind us, as if we were sailing in some gigantic pool of white mud. At the narrowest point the open lead was now only twelve feet wide, and when the bows of the ship nosed into the gap, it quickly became apparent that, in her light, unloaded condition, even under full power, the *Theron* could neither break nor move very heavy ice. We had to go astern and then edge our way forward through the open leads—no easy matter, because the sludge of rafted ice lay behind us and held the individual floes like a liquid cement. Should this 'cement' freeze solid, the ship would be as immobile as if she were set in concrete.

At last Captain Marø was able to start making his way through the complicated maze of closely packed floes to the north, but in less than half an hour, and only two miles from Shackleton, we became immovably jammed and were compelled to settle down to wait for the pressure to ease. The tension on board could be felt, for we all knew that we had to free ourselves quickly, or follow the drift of Shackleton's ill-fated *Endurance*, which was crushed to pieces in the ice. Two hours later we were able to make slow and laborious progress—but it was clear that we had left Shackleton only just in time.

During the night we gradually worked our way to easier conditions near the Caird coast, and on the evening of 8th February we were back at Halley Bay. Stopping only long enough to pick up the Royal Society Expedition's mail, we reached the open sea on 10th February, and sent the following message to our Patron, Her Majesty the Queen:

Expedition vessel *Theron* now clear of Weddell Sea ice on return voyage having established Shackleton Base in latitude 77°57'S, 37°17'W. Wintering Party will examine mountains discovered to the south-east. Loyal greetings to our Queen and Patron.

Fuchs.

We received the following reply:

Thank you for your message. I have been following your adventure with great interest and we are all delighted at your success. Please send my best wishes to all members of your Expedition.

Elizabeth R.

4. The first winter

We left a forlorn little party standing at the ice edge waving their last farewells—they looked puny and insignificant as the *Theron* sailed away, breaking their last link with the outside world. The task ahead of them was formidable, but they were full of confidence and their spirits were high as they turned to challenge the vast icy continent. Winter was coming on—already, with the ship only a mile away, the pack ice was closing solidly against the landing site where she had been moored. But they hoped that in six weeks their hut would be built and that a relatively comfortable winter lay ahead.

They turned back to face the three hundred tons of stores still stacked at the foot of the ice shelf—25 tons of anthracite, 350 barrels of fuel, hutting and boat gear, food, clothing, sledging rations for men and dogs, frozen seals—it looked a picture of utter confusion, and now there were only eight of them to deal with it.

Their first need was to establish themselves securely and to organize their daily existence. Already the temperature was below zero. Up at Shackleton they pitched four two-man pyramid tents around the crate and unpacked sleeping bags and personal gear. Laying a rubber groundsheet on the snow floor in each tent, they covered them with sheepskin rugs, and laid out their sleeping bags. Each tent was supplied with a Primus stove, a hurricane lamp, paraffin, candles and matches.

Presently there was the first 'brew-up' of tea and something to eat inside the crate, then Ralph Lenton and Hannes La Grange started making it drift-proof by covering the outside with roofing felt. Their only furniture was an odd assortment of packing cases and at midnight Taffy Williams kept the first of his regular radio schedules or 'skeds' with the *Theron*. She was about twenty miles away and still visible as he assembled the small hand-cranked transmitter near the entrance to the crate, using a vertical aerial. Five minutes later they could hear the radio officer of the *Theron* calling them, but all their efforts to make it a two-way contact failed and after half an hour the 'watch' was closed down; they all went wearily to bed.

On the second day the more powerful wireless equipment in the Sno-Cat was used for the routine sked with the *Theron*. Again reception was good; they heard John Lewis calling and took down the message he broadcast, but could not make themselves heard. Later in the evening they drove the Sno-Cat to Shackleton and tried to contact the ship from there, but with no result. By the fourth day the *Theron* had sailed out of range. In addition to these 'skeds', Taffy was also constantly listening in and trying to break into the radio conversations between Port Stanley and the Falkland Islands Dependencies Survey bases on the Graham Land Peninsula, but always without success.

For the first ten days the Advance Party's main job was to move stores from the sea ice up to Shackleton, and they realized ruefully that lack of manpower was going to be a very serious problem. The vehicles gave trouble from the start and on the second day Roy Homard and Rhino Goldsmith spent all their time dealing with mechanical troubles. With Ralph and Hannes working inside the crate and Taffy installing his radio equipment, there were only three men left to handle the heavy cases. The available manpower varied from day to day, but they usually managed to move between ten and fifteen tons and after ten days slogging, all the food, the timbers for the hut, fifty barrels of paraffin and petrol and a quantity of general stores and scientific equipment had been hauled up to the base. They then turned their attention to laying the foundations of the hut.

The chosen area of snow was levelled and on this they put down a 'carpet' of expanded metal which would prevent the finished building from sinking into the snow; over this they laid the heavy timber foundations. The whole operation took a fortnight and they began to realize that it would be a good deal longer than six weeks before the roof was on. Taffy renewed his efforts to establish radio contact, but at this time of year radio conditions in the Antarctic are often poor and with the limited power at his disposal all attempts failed.

Next, the heavy trusses which would form the main framework of the hut were hauled upright. This was heavy work, requiring everybody's assistance, but their spirits rose as truss after truss was hoisted into position and their home took shape. Often snow fell, burying their tools, and now the days were getting much shorter, giving them all a sense of urgency to work longer hours and always faster, in order to move into a warm hut before winter and its long darkness overtook them. Bolts, nails and screws were hammered and screwed home merrily as the husky pups, now growing up fast, fought and gambolled around them.

The trusses were built in two halves, and when those on one side were in position, they looked curiously like a row of the 'Queen's Beasts', each waiting for its counterpart to be erected and the two bolted together.

The living quarters in the Sno-Cat crate were assuming an atmosphere of home. The crate was 21′ × 9′ × 8′ and there was now a long, narrow table down the centre with benches on either side. Ralph had built a kitchen shelf across one end, on which stood the three Primus stoves used for cooking and their pots and pans, while the other end was turned into the radio-room-cum-workshop. Here Taffy installed his little transmitter, with the accumulators on a shelf underneath, the remaining space being taken up by tools which, as the temperature dropped, were often found frozen to the wood on which they lay. A door had been cut into the east end, and to give protection from the weather they built a lean-to around this.

The heat from the Primus stoves usually maintained a temperature of about 25°F at waist level, and lines were strung across the ceiling on which socks, gloves and mittens could be dried out; but at ground level it was always very cold and ice an inch thick soon formed all over the floor.

As February advanced they usually started work in the morning in temperatures between zero and −20°F—some thirty to fifty degrees of frost. Occasionally blizzards blew for a whole day, covering the working site and burying the timber, which wasted a lot of time when everything had to be dug out. To handle the nuts and bolts they had to work with bare hands, and they suffered much from frostbitten fingers.

At the beginning of March the weather got worse and blinding drift obliterated everything—these conditions were repeated day after day in the weeks and months to come. Their great enemy was the wind—relentlessly it blew, often at more than twenty knots and always driving a torrent of snow like a horizontal waterfall, filling every nook and cranny, and burying everything in its path. Life consisted almost entirely of digging—cases of food, barrels of fuel, the building timbers, tools, their sleeping tents—nothing escaped, and after a time the drift accumulated faster than they could clear it, so instead of digging down for what they needed, they began to 'tunnel' for their stores and gradually a complete warren was developed. Very often they were not absolutely sure where to tunnel for what they wanted and they could dig and probe all day without success—it was discouraging for they were losing the race against the winter. Some weeks later the tunnels were deliberately extended and used to house the dogs when complete darkness fell and the cold and wind became too severe for them to remain outside.

Meanwhile the dogs were still down on the sea ice where they had been tethered when first they came off the ship. They were not yet trained to run in teams and to walk each animal up to the base separately would have taken a lot of time, so Ken Blaiklock decided to leave them chained to their steel wire spans, and attaching each end to a vehicle, he and Roy drove gaily to the top of the ice shelf, running the dogs up to Shackleton in a chorus of howling excitement. There they were picketed close to the building site, but when the men went back to fetch their winter food supply of seals, huge drifts of soft snow had formed on the steep slope to the top of the ice shelf and the vehicles could not haul the heavily laden sledges over this.

On 1st March the three 'met' men, Tony Stewart, Hannes La Grange and Peter Jeffries, began regular meteorological observations every three hours between 9 a.m. and midnight.

By the 19th of the month the main framework of the hut was up, the gable ends were being completed and the party began to haul the crates of wall panels into position beside the building. But on the 20th what came to be known as 'The Great

March Blizzard' struck them—and was to alter their whole lives.

The day was cloudy, with drifting snow and a light wind, but this gradually increased to thirty knots and the builders were forced to give up their work and seek the shelter of the crate. Except for feeding the dogs, taking the meteorological observations and of course crawling out to their sleeping tents at night, the blizzard held them prisoner in the crate for nine days.

By this time they had settled down to a routine in their tiny home and while the wind howled around them and snow poured into the half-built hut, they spent their time writing, reading, or playing Scrabble. High drifts formed around the vehicles, the tents, and the crate itself—the dogs curled up miserably into tight little balls, wrapping their bushy tails around their faces— Shackleton was indeed a scene of desolation. The time passed slowly, the snow building up outside the door and having to be dug away every hour to prevent them from becoming completely buried.

During this period of inactivity they had time to practise and improve their cooking. Everyone hated this chore and for the first six weeks after the ship left them, their meals were governed by the lack of an oven for baking. Once the original supply of bread was finished, they lived on sledging biscuit, which is like ship's

biscuit but more nourishing. In time, however, the inventive
Roy Homard made an oven from an empty five-gallon BP oil
drum which he insulated with Fibreglass. This was placed on top
of a Primus and became a constant challenge to the duty cook, for
now it was possible to bake bread and make cakes and puddings.
At first they were not very good, but appetites were so keen that
many a burnt offering was scraped and eaten. Later in the winter
when they were not so hungry they became much more 'choosey',
but by then the cooks had mastered their craft and they were
planning to publish a cookery book to be called 52 *Ways of
Cooking Corned Beef*!

Ralph was acknowledged to be the best cook amongst them,
but it was Roy who scored a bullseye by providing tinned peas
with a delicious flavour of mint. Jealously he guarded his secret—
but one day he was seen adding half an inch of Mentasol tooth-
paste to the boiling pot.

Each man cooked for four days at a time and during this period
he was allowed to sleep on the table in the crate, which gave him
a chance to dry out his sleeping bag. But all through the Great
Blizzard the other seven had to journey out each evening to the
tents, clambering over the newly formed 'humps' while the tiny
particles of drift swirled around them, stinging their faces like a
million pin-pricks. Their eyelashes froze and their hands became

dead and frostbitten as the tent flaps were hurriedly undone and they crawled thankfully in. There they would light the Primus stove and begin thawing out their sleeping bags. These were by now sodden with condensation and each day they froze solid, creaking and cracking as their owners tried to open them up. It often took as much as two hours to get them soft enough to crawl into fully clothed.

At last, during the evening of 26th March, the blizzard died away and they were able to move about outside and take stock of the changed scene around them. The shell of the hut was almost clear of snow except for drifts which had gathered against the sacks of bolts stacked down the centre. Once these had become buried, the force of the wind had swept through the trusses taking the drift with it. But to the north and south side of the hut, close to the building, a huge drift seventy yards long stood fifteen feet above the surface, and underneath this lay all the wall panels which had so laboriously been dug out the day before the blizzard began. It was a cruel set-back to their building programme, and hopes of 'moving-in' receded even further. The tents too were almost buried and had to be dug out and re-pitched.

More dog food was needed so Ken Blaiklock and Tony Stewart started down to the sea ice to fetch it. As they reached the top of the slope they were horrified to see clouds of frost-smoke rolling away to the north. Arriving at the stores dump their worst fears were confirmed—the ice which had looked so solid had broken away clean through the middle of the various piles of cases, most of which had disappeared into the open sea. Gone were 300 drums of fuel, a Ferguson tractor, all their coal, the timber for the engineering workshop they had hoped to build, the boat and boat gear, most of the seal carcases and a great many engineering stores. It was a bitter blow indeed. All that was left was some dog pemmican, the sledge ration boxes, a case of detonators and a few drums of cement, one literally teetering on the very edge of the ice.

With this depressing news they made their way gloomily back to base, where Ken immediately called a council of war to discuss their plight. Luckily all the food was up at Shackleton—they had enough for three years in case the relief ship was unable to get back in the 1956–7 season—so their main anxiety would be the quantity of fuel they now had left. They estimated that for both cooking and heating there would be three gallons of paraffin a day for the remainder of the year, and sufficient petrol to use their vehicles sparingly; so, on this basis, they now reorganized their lives to a new routine of careful economy. There could be no question of washing or laundrywork, but the cook's hands remained reasonably clean doing the washing up!

This was perhaps their worst day—but there was still one more blow in store. In the afternoon 'Kusie', one of the favourite huskies, died from exposure. She had clearly been unwell, for instead of lying down like the other dogs, she had remained standing in the blizzard. Seeing her distress, they had brought her into the shelter of the lean-to, providing her with a bed of straw and several hot-water bottles. The men took turns to nurse her, but after moaning piteously for several hours she died, leaving them to care for her five puppies.

Among the stores they had lost were all the chemicals needed for making hydrogen. The meteorologists had planned to carry out radio-sonde work—that is, to let off a balloon each day with instruments attached to it from which a great deal could be learnt about weather conditions in the upper atmosphere. Without hydrogen the balloons could not be inflated and so, to their great disappointment, this programme of work had to be abandoned.

An immediate reaction to their losses was that Taffy now spent many hours each evening plugging away at the 'key' of his radio transmitter trying to pass a message, but still no one picked up his calls. Their nearest neighbours at Halley Bay were listening for him regularly with some anxiety but no contact was made; Taffy was becoming greatly concerned, if not alarmed, at this failure to get in touch with the outside world.

April saw the daylight getting shorter and shorter. The walls of the hut were up and they began fitting the roof panels. This entailed tacking felt to the side of each panel to ensure completely drift-proof joints and was very cold work indeed in sometimes more than sixty-two degrees of frost. It was a difficult job in silk gloves, and impossible when wearing any other form of protection, so they found it quicker to use bare hands for a minute or two at a time, afterwards warming them over a Tilley lamp sheltered in a deep box, provided for this purpose.

Tunnelling for the buried cases was still a tremendous task, but better than digging down through fifteen feet of hard-packed snow, only to have the hole filled in by the next day of drift. On 20th April the sun set for the last time—four months of complete darkness had come, and still they were sleeping in tents.

They continued building whenever the weather permitted but found it impossible to work exposed to the wind when the temperature fell below —45°F, seventy-seven degrees below freezing point. Every day each man set out to his roof panelling or tunnelling carrying his own Tilley lamp; and once a month, if they were lucky and there was not too much cloud, the moon rose, shedding her cold light, which was a help to them in their constant struggle with the weather.

May was their coldest month when temperatures in the minus sixties occurred, and during the first half another blizzard raged, lasting ten days, during which nothing but essential work could be done outside. The dogs still had to be fed, the weather observations taken and food and fuel brought into the crate, while the short journey to the tents each night became more and more unpleasant. The direction of the wind caused the drift to block the entrances and the weary sleepers had to dig their way in. Next morning the duty cook, who had slept inside the crate, went round each tent in turn digging out the occupants for breakfast.

Roy had rigged up a wind generator so at last they had electric light in the crate. Rhino was studying 'human acclimatization to cold' and for this programme his companions acted as guinea-pigs. He measured the amount of calories contained in the food they ate; the clothing they wore and the hours they slept were all faithfully recorded; and once every month each man stripped completely, lying on the table with a lamp shining on him to keep him moderately warm, while Rhino measured his fat thickness.

On 7th May, after twelve weeks of continual effort, it was Ralph Lenton who at last succeeded in making the first radio contact. He had been fiddling with the 'key' trying various frequencies, when suddenly he jumped up, waving his arms and shouting excitedly, 'I've got him! I've got him!' A friend of his at the base on Horseshoe Island, a thousand miles to the north-west, had picked up his signal and was answering. Everyone was spellbound, crowding round the little set, while Ralph returned to the 'key' and started sending their first message. It was a great moment after so many tribulations, and their spirits soared. Soon a telegram was being relayed to London telling us that they were all right.

From that day they were able to establish fairly regular communications—either through Horseshoe Island or Port Stanley in the Falkland Islands, though it was still impossible to speak to Halley Bay, only two hundred miles away. Due to their limited resources and the uncertain radio conditions, contact was possible for only a short time each day, and soon their radio frequency became choked as messages began to pour into the tiny crate. The transmitter which had been only an ornament for so long now proved itself and behaved magnificently. Depending on the temperature, it was either running with water, or covered in frost and ice, making the controls difficult to turn—but still it worked.

Every Tuesday the B.B.C. broadcast personal messages to each of the party in turn. For these occasions the receiver was dismantled, each unit thoroughly dried and then protected from damp until the time of the broadcast. Reception was often not very good, but with eight men glued round the speaker comparing notes afterwards, all the personal messages were understood. The flow of incoming messages cheered them immensely, and even the eternal digging and shovelling away of snow and their painfully slow progress in building the hut could not dampen their spirits.

So ended May, and they began digging their way into June with the drift pouring into the hut almost as fast as they could clear it; on the 6th the wind reached seventy knots. By the time they had removed eighty tons of hard-packed snow from the east end of the hut, another forty tons had filled the west end—it was hard, gruelling work; eight men always fighting a losing battle against drift.

In the Antarctic, Christmas falls right in the middle of the sledging season when everyone is busy and many travellers are away from base, so 21st June—Midwinter Day—is traditionally the great festival, marking the day when the sun begins **its**

slow return. At Shackleton it was declared a holiday, the first they had taken, and despite their discomforts they determined to celebrate in style. Radio greetings had been pouring in from all over the world, Ralph undertook to prepare a meal worthy of the occasion, and they brought out all the presents from home which had been carefully kept for this day. For the midday feast their table was for once graced with a cloth and a large Dundee cake formed a centre-piece, round which a small clockwork train, presented by the staff of the Scott Polar Research Institute, ran endlessly on its tiny rails. Above it they placed a set of Christmas 'Angel Chimes' from one of their parcels, and two golden angels revolved slowly in the warmth of the candles, merrily tinkling tiny bells. The menu included turtle soup, ham with Brussels sprouts and fresh bread rolls, followed by strawberry shortcake and tinned cream.

They had even made presents for each other, and Peter Jeffries, who read throughout his meals, received a book-marker inscribed '*Here you were interrupted. . . .*' There were crackers and paper hats, balloons, games, sweets, cigars, and numerous musical instruments that added to the air of gaiety, helping them to forget for a time their isolation and the perpetual battle with wind and the ever encroaching drift. It was a fine 'do'.

Next day they were out as usual with shovels, digging away snow from the framework of the hut so that Ralph could begin to set up the interior partitions. By the end of the month the eastern half was taking shape and had been sealed off with snow blocks so that work could continue inside whatever the weather. It was very cold work and because paraffin was rationed, they used a makeshift brazier which provided warmth for numbed fingers by burning the building scraps and boxwood. The ceiling became blackened and often the clouds of smoke would be too much for the chilled workers, who had to seek fresh air in the snow-filled west end of the hut when the fumes became overpowering.

On 15th July Taffy was at last able to make a brief radio contact with Halley Bay. Soon after that radio conditions gradually improved and many happy evenings were spent at both bases 'having a maunder' or swapping news. By the end of the month their eyes were constantly turned to the northern horizon, searching for the first faint glimmer of light which would herald the return of the sun. On 2nd August they recorded their lowest temperature, —63°F, or ninety-five degrees of frost. In London David Stratton was getting married. This was a big occasion for the Expedition and the Advance Party were determined to share in our celebrations, but alas! at Shackleton even the whisky froze and the paraffin turned into a jelly.

When the ship left them on 7th February, they had planned to take six weeks to build their hut. Exactly six months later, the first two occupants, Ken and Rhino, moved in. Many of the bunks had now been installed, but with the loss of their coal it was much easier to warm the tents and people were disinclined to give them up. Soon the Aga cooker was erected, but remained purely ornamental until the relief ship could bring them fuel; tables, chairs and mattresses were also unpacked and a floor covering put down. The hut was beginning to look like a home.

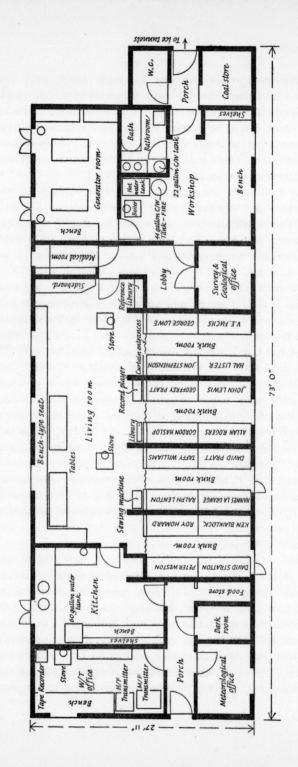

SHACKLETON BASE HUT PLAN

A partial daylight began to appear, raising their spirits and giving a new impetus to the outside work. Roy got one of the Weasels going and this was now used to move heavy material about the base site. The dogs were brought out from the tunnels and dog training began. On 23rd August the sun came back.

With more and more hours of daylight it really felt as if winter was passing and spring was on the way; but even when the whole party finally abandoned the crate which had been their home for eight months and moved into the hut, the outside temperature was still −40°F. To celebrate their move they collected waste wood from the empty packing cases and lit a fire in the hut stove, everyone rushing outside to watch the first smoke coming from the chimney.

The dogs were again picketed outside and were taken for training runs. Only a few weeks' dog food remained and on 29th September, hoping that the seals had returned, Ken and Rhino took one team down to Vahsel Bay. They brought back as much meat as they could haul, and had seen enough seals to know that they could fetch in sufficient to feed the dogs until the relief ship arrived in January.

It was time to install the large diesel generators and the main radio transmitter which would make possible direct communication with the General Post Office in England. All this heavy equipment was buried deep in drift and they had to dig a huge hole six feet deep and twenty-five feet across, before the cases could be hauled out with a Weasel and towed over to the hut. At the same time Taffy was busy erecting four 52-foot tall masts which would carry the special aerial for communication with the United Kingdom.

By the end of October the generators and the transmitter were working and on the 29th they established direct voice contact with the B.B.C. in London. Reception was very clear and several 'tests' were made on consecutive days in preparation for the first radio programme about the expedition which would include the voices of those at Shackleton. During these tests the B.B.C. allowed members of the Expedition in London to be in the studio to talk to the party at base, and we all greatly enjoyed these opportunities of telling them our plans and exchanging news.

At the end of October the spring journeys began. First Ken,

Roy and Hannes, with one dog team and a Weasel, left to hunt more seals in Vahsel Bay. They covered thirty-two miles in less than nine hours and were back at Shackleton the following night with 1½ tons of meat. By November the sun was again shining for the full twenty-four hours and according to their standards of temperature it was 'gloriously warm'. At last clothes were washed and bodies scrubbed, using water heated on their wood-burning stove in buckets and bowls.

It was time to start the southern dog sledge journeys which would find a route for our vehicles on the first stage of the crossing of the continent the next season. Ken, Rhino and Peter made two short trips to establish a depot fifty miles south of Shackleton. Then, on 7th December, Ken and Rhino, with one dog team, set out for the Theron Mountains, which we had seen from the air in February. Picking up supplies from 50-Mile Depot, they travelled southwards over the flat, monotonous ice shelf, finding large holes here and there and some crevasses, but nothing to trouble dog sledges. They were making for a single rocky peak that peered over the horizon day after day, never seeming to come any closer, so they called it 'Mount Faraway'.

The weather was fine, with brilliant sunshine, and the temperature rose to the plus twenties, the snow becoming so soft that they changed to night travel when the colder conditions provided a harder surface for the sledges. They covered fifteen to sixteen miles daily, reporting their position back to base every third evening. After eleven days they camped at last at the foot of Mount Faraway; here they fixed their position by the sun, and then collected many interesting rock specimens which showed the Theron Mountains to be composed of sandstones, shales and limestones.

Turning back with eight days' food left and 120 miles to cover to reach 50-Mile Depot, they had a difficult run in soft snow and bad weather but arrived on Christmas Day. To celebrate, the dogs got an extra block of pemmican, while for the men the depot stores provided a 'believe-it-or-not' sort of meal of soup, smoked salmon, asparagus, and pineapple glacé—which was a welcome change from the monotonous ration of pemmican. Two days later, having covered 360 miles in twenty days, they were back at base.

By New Year's Day the relief ship *Magga Dan* was already in the Weddell Sea, and soon the Main Party would arrive at Shackleton, bringing with us fresh supplies and a year's mail from home. In spite of living in very cramped quarters, of sleeping a polar winter in tents at latitude 78°S, and enduring much greater hardships than might reasonably have been expected, the Advance Party had performed their tasks and the first phase of the expedition had been successfully completed. They had built the hut for us, and the first part of the route to the south had been reconnoitred over the ground. Now they would be reinforced with more men, more vehicles and more stores—ready to face the second winter and prepare for the crossing of the continent. We were grateful for all they had done.

5. *South Ice*

The *Theron* brought us back to London on 23rd
March 1956. The next six months were spent obtaining more
stores and equipment and preparing for our final return to
Shackleton and the Advance Party at the end of the year. The
three additional Sno-Cats came from America and were taken
over to Norway to be tested in the Jotunheim mountains. A de
Havilland Otter, a single-engined, high-wing monoplane, was
bought in Canada and flown via Greenland to England by John
Lewis and Gordon Haslop. By October an endless stream of stores
was once more being assembled and packed, ready for shipment.

During the summer the last four members of the Expedition
joined. Dr. Hal Lister, a glaciologist who was to command the
inland station during the next Antarctic winter; Dr. Allan
Rogers, a physiologist who was to replace Rhino Goldsmith as our
medical officer for the second season; Dr. Jon Stephenson, an
Australian geologist, and Geoffrey Pratt, a geophysicist lent to us
by the British Petroleum Company. Geoffrey now became
responsible for our seismic work and the gravity traverse we
planned to make across the continent.

At the beginning of November the newly built Danish Polar
vessel, the *Magga Dan*, 1,850 tons, commanded by Captain Hans
Petersen, arrived at Tower Bridge and began loading. We were
to share this ship, twice the size of the little *Theron*, with the
Royal Society Expedition's relief party to Halley Bay.

Although not a true icebreaker, the *Magga Dan* was specially
designed for work in the ice; and very splendid she looked with
her sides painted bright red so as to be easily seen among the
ice floes. Her hull was of steel an inch thick throughout, making
it very strong. Her propeller was of the variable pitch variety so
50

that it was unnecessary to stop and start the engines when going ahead and astern alternately. In the crow's nest, which was reached by climbing up inside the mast, there was a duplicate set of controls and instruments necessary to navigate the ship. Rudder, propeller pitch and engine speed could all be controlled from this point by the helmsman navigating the ship through the ice.

Another feature was the special apparatus for making fresh water. This used no fuel as is normally the case. The heat came from the cooling water of the diesel engines and as much as eleven tons of fresh water could be made in a day—we were therefore saved the heavy task of melting huge quantities of ice, as we had had to do in the *Theron*, besides saving many tons of fuel.

All the generators, engines and pumps were duplicated so that one could be repaired while the other was in use. There was even a separate engine and generator in the forepeak, which could pump out the engine-room if this should be holed by the ice. All this made us very confident about our next attempt to enter the Weddell Sea.

On 13th November her Majesty the Queen inspected the ship and received members of the Expedition. On the 15th we sailed on the 10,000-mile voyage back to Shackleton; again travelling via Montevideo and the island of South Georgia to top up the ship's fuel tanks. Three days before Christmas we again met ice in position 58°38'S, 30°00'W, and soon the *Magga Dan* was cutting her way through brash and bergy bits which gradually gave way to thin, rotten ice. This in turn thickened and increased in size until we were in the pack proper.

One day John Lewis was on deck and suddenly noticed a smell of burning. Looking round he saw wisps of smoke rising from beneath a tarpaulin lashed over one of the ship's electric winches. While someone rushed away to fetch the chief electrician, he tore off the covering and found the entire winch smoking hot owing to an electrical fault. There were six barrels of aviation spirit firmly lashed to it and had these caught fire, the other 650 barrels on deck would certainly have gone up too—with disastrous results!

The Danes celebrate Christmas on 24th December and we

decided that the two expeditions on board would join in their festivities rather than upset the ship's routine twice in twenty-four hours. So at five o'clock the engines were stopped in a convenient lead and we all went to the various messes for our Christmas dinner. On Christmas morning we opened the presents our families had provided and were particularly delighted with a parcel sent by David Stratton's wife, which contained brightly coloured knitted caps and some form of musical instrument for each of us. Before long we were gathered on the after deck wearing our new headgear and experimenting with our instruments—but we were soon appalled at the awful noise we made and they were put away for later use at Shackleton parties. In the afternoon we listened to the Queen's Christmas broadcast, and in the evening the ship made wireless contact with Shackleton and we were able to 'have a Christmas maunder' with the Advance Party.

On Boxing Day John Lewis took the ship's first officer on a reconnaissance flight in the Auster, during which they saw a huge area of open water extending for about a hundred miles to the south of us. On reaching it Captain Petersen set the automatic pilot, probably the first time this has ever been possible in the Weddell Sea. However, our rising hopes of an easy passage faded when we reached 69°43'S, for the stretch of open water we had been following was suddenly closed by solid and impenetrable pack ice. Very soon it looked as if we might be running into real trouble.

The ship was stopped in a pool beside a small iceberg and Gordon Haslop flew the first officer to reconnoitre ahead. On their return they told us that we had to retire ignominiously backwards and try to break east towards some areas of dark *water sky* which indicated more open conditions. But first we had to extricate the ship from the closely packed floes and, as in the previous season, everyone was over the side again, chopping, digging, levering, winching and poling the ice.

On the morning of 30th December John made three separate flights looking for a way out of our difficulties. Finally, by sailing

---

Dark patches in the sky due to the reflection of open water on clouds are known as a *water sky*.

north-east, we were able to free the ship and to find a wide lead which took us into the open belt of water which forms along the Caird coast in the summer. On 4th January we reached Halley Bay.

The next week was a busy one for us all. The Otter was put ashore to have the wings fitted, while three hundred tons of stores were unloaded and taken up to the Royal Society Base. At the same time Geoffrey Pratt made local seismic soundings and gravity observations.

When ready the Otter was tested and we then took the opportunity to fly east from Halley Bay to investigate the possible existence of mountains. After 230 miles we found a fine rocky range where the peaks reached to over nine thousand feet. This new discovery was named after the Norwegian sealer *Tottan*, which had brought the Royal Society Expedition's Advance Party to Halley Bay, but being in Norwegian territory, the name that will appear on the maps is Tottanfjellene, meaning Tottan Mountains.

During the flight back to base we failed to pick up the radio beacon at Halley Bay, so that with our unknown rate of drift to one side in the wind we were soon off course and lost. Presently the engine coughed, then stopped, and knowing from the outward flight that a completely impassable area of crevasses lay between us and Halley Bay, I began to imagine an unpleasant situation if we had to make a forced landing. John Lewis hastily switched to another fuel tank, which was already nearly empty, and the engine started again, but a few minutes later the same thing happened as this tank was also drained dry and John had to start the third and last tank. All this was hardly encouraging—particularly for our photographer George Lowe, and David Dalgliesh and Robin Smart of the Royal Society Expedition who were all in the back of the plane and could not know what was going on. Puzzled by the stopping and starting of the engine, Robin asked George if anything was the matter.

'I don't think they know where we are,' replied George.

'Oh,' said Robin cheerfully. 'In that case I don't think there is anything I can do to help'—and he calmly lay back to admire the view!

John was certain we had drifted south off our course, so he

turned north-north-west hoping to hit the coast and follow it back to the ship. Presently there was a small gap in the clouds through which we could see two ice floes floating on dark water. Down we went through the hole, and found ourselves over heavily crevassed ice cliffs. John's guess was proved right and all we had to do was to fly north along the coast back to base.

Next morning, 12th January 1957, we were ready to leave for Shackleton. The plane was loaded with all the mail for the Advance Party, fresh meat, vegetables, sacks of anthracite for the Aga, potatoes, oranges and apples, and three of us set off with John Lewis. After two hours, flying in clear skies and brilliant sunshine, Shackleton became visible when we were still twenty miles away.

A flagged runway had been marked out and as John circled the base we could see a small group of figures waiting for us. A short distance away rows of tiny black specks showed where the dogs were spanned out on the snow. It was an exciting moment. As the plane came to rest beside the waiting group we jumped out, to receive a great welcome from those we had left behind the previous year. We were happy to see them all looking fit and well.

The stores were unloaded on to a sledge and soon we were all driving over to the hut where the rest of the day was spent by the Advance Party in reading their letters and in exchanging Shackleton news for news of the outside world. Ken Blaiklock took me round the site to see the stores dumps and the general lay-out of the base. The crate in which they had wintered was now derelict and buried to the roof in snow, but it was easy to visualize the appalling conditions in which they had lived. It was late that sunlit night when we all went to bed.

David Stratton reported by radio from the *Magga Dan* that the ship was making good progress on her way from Halley Bay and would arrive the next afternoon. Roy Homard built a bonfire with old packing cases at the edge of the ice shelf, and after lunch this was lit to guide the ship in, while we all went down to the ice edge to watch her arrival. Remembering the storm which had overtaken the *Theron* the year before, Captain Petersen wanted to protect the *Magga Dan* from a similar experience, so he used the ship to cut a small 'dock' by continually driving her into the ice, breaking away huge pieces with every run. After the first hour of this work, we who were waiting on the ice were able to scramble aboard; the shouted greetings quickly turned to handshakes and the Advance Party were soon lost among the various cabins, exchanging news. After four hours the ship was sufficiently into the firm ice to be protected from all but a direct northerly blow, and even then only small floes would be able to follow her into the 'dock'. It was immediately christened 'Pete's Cove'.

So—at last—all the members of the Expedition were together again, ready to complete the building and storing of Shackleton before the ship left. We also had on board the ten members of the Royal Society Expedition's Advance Party who were returning to England, but in the meantime had offered to help us with all the work ahead.

Our first task was to find a site and establish our 900-mile inland station before the winter set in. We still hoped that 'Depot 300' would be set up by a ground party supported by aircraft, for then the vehicle route would be 'proved' before our main journey began in November, but several long-range reconnaissance flights were necessary before the site could be selected.

On 20th January Gordon Haslop took off with Ken Blaiklock, George Lowe and myself as passengers. Leaving the Theron Mountains to the east we flew direct to the larger range farther south which we later called the Shackleton Range. Forty miles from base we passed over a great chasm which we had seen from the air the previous season, and which we knew would be our first major obstacle on the trans-continental journey. During the flight we saw two large glaciers sweeping down between the buried mountain peaks. One we called the Slessor Glacier after Sir John Slessor, Chairman of the Expedition Committee, while the second became known as the Recovery Glacier. Farther south we could see a line of rocky peaks, but at this point we were almost at the limit of our fuel endurance and had to decide which way we would go home—the rocks were therefore known as the *Whichaway Nunataks*. All these features are shown on the map on page 56.

A *nunatak* is a rock mass, often of pyramid form, entirely surrounded by ice and snow. It is usually the top of a buried mountain.

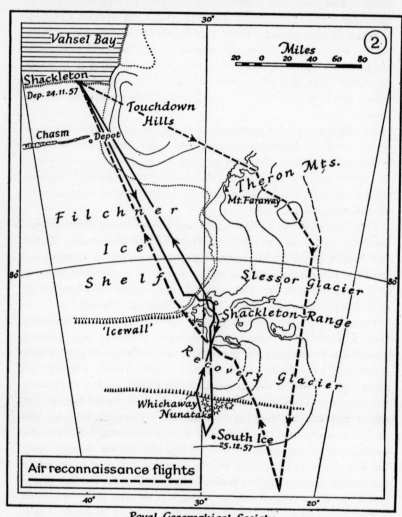

Royal Geographical Society

As a result of this flight we decided to set up Depot 300 about thirty miles beyond the Whichaway Nunataks, but although we had chosen the approximate position, there were many difficult, if not impossible, obstructions on the ground and two more long flights (as shown on the map), were made to enable us to examine the different routes through which it might be possible to get our vehicles on to the polar plateau.

On the first of these, as we were returning to base via the Theron Mountains, we flew along the vertical cliffs towards Mount Faraway. There we could see that the surface below was good enough for a landing. John Lewis brought the Otter down about a mile and a half from a great rock wall towards which I set off on foot at top speed. Among the limestones and shales I found a number of coal seams which were geologically interesting, and could also provide us with extra fuel if we were unlucky enough to be stranded at Shackleton for a year longer than we expected. Hastily I chipped out all the specimens I could carry, and twenty minutes later was back on board and we were again heading for base.

During this time everyone at Shackleton had been working very hard unloading the ship, erecting more buildings and collecting more seal meat for the dogs. Using three Sno-Cats, one Weasel and the Muskeg tractor, we were able to move seventy-five tons of stores a day up to the base. Ralph Lenton and a party of workers from the Royal Society Expedition were completing the hut and had started to put up the other buildings. A hot-water system was being installed and the electric wiring completed. The new buildings consisted of the aircraft workshop, the vehicle stores huts, the hydrogen hut and our emergency stores hut, which was built some distance away as a safety precaution in case of a fire in the base.

When constructing an Antarctic base there is always the problem of what to do with all the material that cannot be brought under cover. Past expeditions have tried building tunnels of the actual packing cases themselves. When these become drifted over with snow, it is possible to walk inside the tunnels and obtain what is wanted by opening the end of the appropriate case. But by this method the surface of the snow is raised to the height of the tunnel and the drift will then extend over an ever widening area, to form ridges and hollows that make movement about the base difficult during the dark winter months.

At Shackleton we had noticed that where there was no obstruction to the wind, the snow blew away and did not accumulate. We therefore laid out our stores and barrels of fuel in long, widely separated lines, and never allowed one case to stand on top of another. In this way the tops of the boxes remained exposed at the surface and we could find and dig up anything we required. By this time the site of the base was quite extensive—from east to west it covered eight hundred yards, from north to south four hundred yards.

By the end of January it was time for the ship to leave us. On the 27th we gave a farewell party at Shackleton for the officers and crew. The highlight of the evening came when Douglas Prior of the Royal Society Expedition, who is a small man, was carried across our crowded living-room and hung by his braces on the corner of the door. There he dangled like a protesting spider from its thread until his struggles released him and he fell on the floor in a confused heap!

Next day was writing day. No work was done, and all those who were staying behind dashed off their last letters. In the evening the ship gave a return party and next morning we all congregated on the ice to see her sail. Slowly she pulled out of Pete's Cove and began to move along the ice edge, her high, raking bow far out of the water, dispersing a school of killer whales as she went. Now we were indeed 'marooned'—for, as in the days of the buccaneers, we had been purposely set down on a desolate coast and no ship would return to pick us up again. Our way out was two thousand miles across a continent of ice. We turned to the vehicles and dog sledges and hastened back to Shackleton and our work.

We soon began to shake down as a single unit, and quickly found that our great problem was going to be manpower. So much to do, so few to do it, everyone competent to perform a number of specialized tasks, but all of them needing to be done at once. Sixteen pairs of hands were not enough.

The season was far advanced and it was clear that there would not be time to prove the ground route inland, and that Depot 300 would therefore have to be put down entirely by air. The next four days were spent in preparing separate loads, each of 2,000 lbs. First came the camping equipment, food, fuel and radio, which would go with the building party on the first flight. Next the hutting material and tools, which had to be packed in the right order, followed by furniture, generators, scientific equipment and personal gear. To save weight every item was unpacked, then weighed and labelled, before being allocated to its flight load.

On 4th February John Lewis took off, with Hal Lister, Ken Blaiklock, Jon Stephenson and George Lowe, together with thirty days' supplies. He put them down in position 81°56′S, 29°30′W, and as soon as the tents were pitched the building party went into action. Their prefabricated hut was sixteen feet square, made of lightweight aluminium, and in order to encourage quick drifting up, which would help to keep it warm, they first dug a pit about five feet deep in which the foundations were laid. Work went on for fifteen hours each day.

From then onwards every opportunity was taken to fly, whether by day or by night, for the weather could not be expected to hold for many weeks and at any season the number of safe flying days is restricted. The distance between Shackleton and the Depot was actually 275 miles by air (it was later to prove very much longer over the ground), and although we now had the advantage of weather reports from the depot itself, conditions could change so quickly that sometimes the plane had to turn back when half-way on the journey.

It took twenty flights to stock the depot completely for the winter and on each flight one or other of us accompanied the pilot, since it would be undesirable for him to be alone with the plane if it were forced down. Sometimes a specialist had a task to perform, such as the erection of the wind generator by Roy Homard, the installation of the radio by Taffy Williams, or the making of gravity observations by Geoffrey Pratt. During my visits to the depot I was able to study the possible surface route in detail, but although in the next season the Crossing Party followed the general line I then selected, we were to find many more areas of trouble than could be seen from the air.

At the end of a fortnight the outer shell of the depot hut had been finished and was already drifted up, with little more than the shining aluminium roof panels and chimneys showing at the surface. The inside partitioning had yet to be completed and the building party were still living in tents. The entrance, which

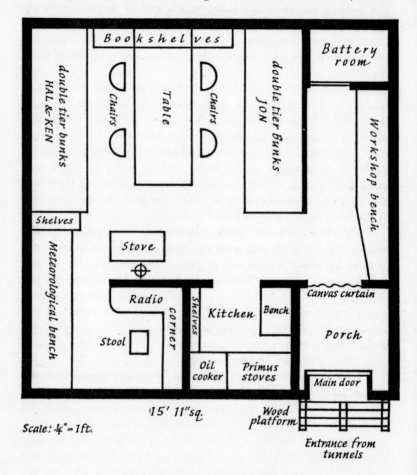

Scale: ¼" = 1ft.

SOUTH ICE HUT PLAN

would ultimately be through a trapdoor, was then down a flight of snow steps; from beside the door a tunnel had been dug to a number of small chambers which would serve as store-rooms, a snow crystal laboratory, the generator room and a lavatory. The station was to be manned during the winter by Hal Lister, Jon Stephenson and Ken Blaiklock. Hal had been a member of the British North Greenland Expedition, when he had spent an isolated Arctic winter at a similar ice-cap station called North Ice. Chiefly because of his 'home from home' feeling, Depot 300 now came to be known as South Ice.

By 22nd February the hut was ready for occupation and two tons of food and ten barrels of paraffin had already been flown in. This meant that the party were safe for the winter, although for their complete comfort they would require a total of thirty-five barrels of paraffin, each weighing 360 lbs., more petrol for their generator and a reserve of aircraft fuel. This would entail many more flights, but now a radio beacon was operating, enabling the plane to find South Ice in bad visibility—while the more powerful radio transmitter provided constant weather reports to Shackleton.

Each of the wintering party was to come back to Shackleton for a few days before they were finally isolated for the next seven months. The first to return was Ken Blaiklock, who flew back with Gordon Haslop on the night of 23rd February. They took off from South Ice at midnight in a temperature of −40°F. Conditions were poor and Gordon had to fly for the last two hundred miles between two layers of cloud. While still forty miles away he reported receiving the Shackleton beacon satisfactorily and said he was going down to find out the height of the lower cloud. Seconds later the skis of the Otter hit the top of some hills at 110 knots and the aircraft bounded upwards—in the poor light the snow-covered hills had so merged with the cloud as to be invisible. Fortunately Gordon was able to regain control and climb away, but both he and Ken arrived back at Shackleton a little shaken by their experience, and ever since the hills extending southward from Vahsel Bay have been known as the Touchdown Hills!

While flying to South Ice continued whenever possible, we also had plenty to do at Shackleton, the major task being the building of the vehicle workshop. Until it was complete none of the power tools could be set up, nor could work on the vehicles be done under cover. This was seriously hampering our engineers, who were already preparing and modifying the vehicles for the journeys ahead. This workshop was a heavily constructed wooden hut to which Ralph Lenton added a small annexe. From the apex of the main structure hung a small travelling hoist which could lift engines or even one end of a Weasel. On the benches and in the annexe were electric drills, grinders, a press and a lathe, the power for which came from the generators in the main hut about two hundred yards away. The doors at one end were large enough to admit a Sno-Cat, and we dug an inspection pit in the floor to permit work under the vehicles.

Until this was finished David Pratt and Roy Homard carried out necessary work in the temporary shelter of an inflatable rubber garage, which folded into the shape of a large suitcase and weighed 120 lbs. The fabric walls of the garage were attached to a framework of rubber tubes which became rigid when inflated. With a small electric motor we could blow them up in three or four minutes and then it stood thirty feet long, fifteen feet wide and nine feet high—four men could pick it up quite easily. It had one curious and uncanny characteristic. When the sun was high its warmth heated the air inside the garage and it stood up firm and rigid, but as the sun sank and the air cooled, it shrank and slowly collapsed, enveloping any vehicle it contained. Next morning, in warmer conditions, we would find it again fully erect, ready for the engineers to continue their tasks.

Before the winter closed in Ken Blaiklock and Jon Stephenson were most anxious to do survey and geological work in the Whichaway Nunataks, so on 3rd March they were flown there and set down with rations for ten days, a small sledge and a radio receiver, expecting to be picked up again three days later. On the 6th Gordon and I took off from Shackleton, but South Ice reported that the weather there had deteriorated and we had to turn back.

Three days later we were still grounded and getting anxious. Every two hours we had a radio schedule with South Ice, hoping for a favourable weather report. That night Ken and Jon would have had four days' rations left and I estimated that the following day they would probably start manhauling their sledge the thirty miles back to South Ice. With the temperatures now constantly below — 40°F and winds up to thirty knots, this would not be a pleasant experience, and they would also have the problem of navigation in the drifting snow. In such conditions they could pass within fifty or a hundred yards of the depot without seeing it, and I told South Ice to fire a recognition signal every night at six o'clock in case the field party needed guidance.

At last, on 11th March, South Ice reported clear skies but very heavy drift on the ground. Gordon and I immediately left Shackleton in the Otter, hoping to be able to pick up the Whichaway party, or at least to drop them more food and fuel. We had sewn the rations up tightly in sacks with red streamers attached to them. We left at midday in perfect conditions, but flying over the Recovery Glacier the whole surface was hidden by snaking, writhing streams of drift which seemed to have a stealthy, veil-like appearance.

Arriving at the nunataks we circled the spot where Ken and Jon had been left but there was no sign of them or their camp. Round and round we went, searching the vicinity of every nunatak for half an hour, but it was no good and we set course for South Ice. Below us streamed the rippling drift, but weaving from side to side to cover as much ground as possible, we searched the route looking vainly for our friends, or at least a sign or the shape of a tent.

Soon we were over South Ice and circling to descend. From above the hut was clearly visible, but as we ran in to land the surface completely disappeared. Then in a flash we were flying through a torrent of snow which obscured everything as effectively as the blackest night. Gingerly we felt our way down, hoping for the best, until the skis touched and Gordon brought us bounding gently over the *sastrugi* to a standstill.

We could see nothing at all through the white wall of swirling snow, but could talk to South Ice over our radio and I asked them to fire a 'two star red' rocket to give some indication of the direction of the hut. There was a little delay as Hal had trouble lighting it in the strong wind, but suddenly we could see a trail of smoke blowing away high above the fifty-foot drift which enveloped us. At once Gordon tried to taxi towards it, only to find that the skis had become frozen to the surface.

Sastrugi are fluted ridges carved by the wind from a snow surface. They may be from a few inches to five feet high and are so hard that a man walking on them will leave no footprint.

He stopped the engine and we fitted the wind baffle and exhaust plugs to conserve as much heat as possible, for the temperature was $-25°F$ and the wind speed thirty-five knots. To lessen the weight we then unloaded the 1,500 lbs. of fuel barrels which we had brought, and I walked forward in the hope of being able to see the South Ice wireless masts. All the time it was necessary to keep looking behind to make sure the plane remained in sight, because once lost it would be only too for me to lose my way altogether. After fifty yards it disappeared so I was forced to turn back.

Removing the wind baffles, we climbed in again and with less weight on board Gordon was able to start taxi-ing cautiously forward. We did not want to run into masts, stores dumps or the hut itself, and it was important not to overshoot the depot as it would be quite impossible to turn the plane round in such a wind.

Presently a lumbering figure stumbled out of the drift, waving heavily muffled arms; this proved to be Hal Lister, who had ploughed over towards the sound of the engine. He shouted that he could not wait as his footprints would quickly be drifted up and he needed these to find his way back to South Ice, two hundred yards distant. I therefore jumped out and ran back with him, talking while making new footprints, until we found David Stratton standing within sight of the hut. Hastily we all three ran back to the plane and held a hurried consultation while I handed over two frozen chickens we had brought for them, before they had to chase their footprints back to the hut.

As soon as we heard David on the radio again, Gordon made an 'instrument take-off'. As we flew the sun sank below the horizon and, for the first time, we landed along a flare path at base. Everyone was very concerned that we had not found Ken and Jon for now they would have only two days' full rations left. However, we hoped that as the bad weather persisted, they had saved a little food each day and finally gone on to half rations.

The weather made a second relief flight impossible until the 15th—two days after their food should have been finished. Early that morning South Ice reported excellent conditions, and by 4.30 a.m. John Lewis, Geoffrey Pratt and I were airborne. There was thick cloud cover over the Theron Mountains and the Shackleton Range, and over the Recovery Glacier we flew at 300

feet but could still see nothing. Then far ahead, a small black
peak appeared which we knew must be the highest of the Whichaway Nunataks. By some miracle the cloud had dispersed around
the nunataks, and they were clearly displayed before us. Presently
we could see that, even more miraculously, the cloud-free area
extended a solitary arm in the direction of South Ice, while
everything else remained under a thick woolly, blanket.

The sun shone brightly on the snow where Ken and Jon had been put down, enabling us to see the empty ration boxes left at their camp site. Thinking that they would have left a note, we went down, John making a skilful landing on a surface torn by the recent winds. In a ration box we found a message telling us that they had left at 11 a.m. on 11th March—five days previously—with four days' full rations and two days' emergency rations. They also gave precise directions concerning the route they intended to follow.

Leaving behind ten days' rations and four gallons of paraffin so that if we failed to find them they could be told by radio where to go for food, we climbed back into the Otter and started to search along the route they had given. Although visibility was excellent we still saw nothing by the time we were circling South Ice. Before landing to refuel we decided to make one more run. This time, while scanning the snow with binoculars, I saw a tiny black triangle in the vast white expanse, about twelve miles from South Ice. It could only be their tent!

In a moment we had turned to fly towards it; then we were bounding over the snow and came to rest fifteen yards from the little camp. Just as we landed I saw Ken's half-dressed figure come out and, as the temperature was −35°F, quickly go back inside. Leaping out of the plane I went over and put my head inside the tent where I found them both well, seemingly unconcerned by their circumstances, and drinking a cup of cocoa which they insisted they finish before dressing to come outside.

While they got ready, Geoffrey and I stowed all their camping gear and sledge in the Otter. Fifteen minutes later we were all on our way back to South Ice where Hal and David Stratton had prepared a very welcome hot breakfast. Afterwards we were able to examine our wanderers and found that Jon was frostbitten on nose, cheeks, both heels and one finger. Ken had got off more lightly, with frostbite of the finger-tips.

We learned that each day they had marched for six hours, towing their sledge in the teeth of winds varying from twenty to thirty-five knots, in conditions of severe drift with the temperature ranging from −25°F to −47°F, covering five or six miles over steeply undulating country. When we found them they still had half rations for one day and one more fill of paraffin for the

Primus. That day they had determined to keep going till they reached South Ice, regardless of how long it took. We were relieved that it had not been necessary.

Deciding to take them both back to Shackleton to recuperate, I asked Geoffrey to remain at South Ice with Hal for a few days until they were fit enough to return.

During this period of anxiety, while we were having lunch at Shackleton, there was a sudden cry of 'Fire!' in the living-room and smoke could be seen pouring from the attic. David Pratt leapt up the ladder to the roof while the rest of us rushed to the workshop where a sheet of flame was shooting up the wall behind the bathroom boiler into the roof. As Roy Homard hurled a bucket of water on to the flames below, David let off a nitrogen pressurized powder extinguisher from above. In a moment the fire was out—and seconds later so was the Expedition, as the air filled with choking dust and we spluttered our way to open all the doors. Happy to find how efficient our specially constructed extinguisher had proved, we all sat down again to a powder-covered lunch, the only complaint coming from Dr. Allan Rogers, who was worrying in case the powder might prove harmful. However we all ate the food, powder and all—even the doctor—and no one was any the worse.

On 22nd, 23rd and 25th March the last three flights to South Ice were made; Ken and Jon returned to join Hal Lister for the winter, the others coming back to Shackleton. On the occasion of the last flight we could only think of three mapping nibs, a bottle of ink, a bottle of photographic developer and a 12-inch ruler to add to the main load of five drums of paraffin. Now the little depot was fully equipped for eight months, for we had provisioned it with sufficient stores to last until it was abandoned by the trans-continental party the following November.

6. The first summer at Scott Base

Whilst we who had returned to London in the *Theron* were preparing to go south again, the Ross Sea Committee in New Zealand were working equally hard recruiting and obtaining the stores and equipment for the party which would set up Scott Base in McMurdo Sound, on the opposite side of the Antarctic continent to Shackleton. Out of more than five hundred applicants, eighteen men were chosen, among them two English members, Dr. George Marsh, who would be the medical officer, and Lieutenant Richard Brooke of the Royal Navy, a surveyor. Both of them had had Antarctic experience and were therefore able to train the dog teams and teach the New Zealanders how to handle them.

The party was to be equipped with a single-engined Beaver aircraft for supplying the depots, a little Auster for reconnaissance, and five small Ferguson tractors. But it was planned that the main field journeys would be made with dog teams, and so sixty huskies were assembled up in the snows of the Tasman Glacier under the care of Harry Ayres, one of the dog handlers. Then when George Marsh arrived, he spent most of the summer training the teams.

During August and September Ed Hillary took his whole party nine miles up the glacier where, at an altitude of 5,500 feet, they underwent a thorough training. All their supplies were flown in by the two aircraft, and the first ski-landings provided many anxious moments—indeed the Auster's first landing was also its last. The combined ski and wheel landing gear specially developed for it proved unsatisfactory, and as John

Claydon brought it down, the ski tips caught in the snow and the plane turned a half-somersault on its nose and landed flat on its back. Fortunately John was unhurt and the aircraft was turned upright and dragged to the shelter of some snow hummocks, where a protective wall of snow blocks was built around it. Here it was repaired and standard aircraft skis were substituted for the offending ski-wheels—all in blizzard conditions, which was good practice for the airmen who would have to operate and maintain the plane in the Antarctic.

The Beaver also had trouble on its initial landing but the fault was soon found and put right. The plane was then used to carry large quantities of stores up the glacier and the flights provided an excellent opportunity for the men to gain experience in ground-to-air communications.

All of them learnt how to handle dog teams and sledging equipment, while a radio was installed in the Malte Brun Hut on the Glacier and the operators maintained daily communication with Wellington, where one of the main Scott Base radio sets had been temporarily set up. Those with no previous mountaineering experience were taught how to use an ice-axe, while everyone did a lot of ski-ing and learnt to drive the tractors. Their cook, Sel Bucknel, went with them and worked hard to appease very keen appetites with the aid of three Primus stoves.

The New Zealand Government generously provided H.M.N.Z.S. *Endeavour* (Captain Harry Kirkwood, Royal Navy), a small wooden net-layer, to carry the New Zealand Party to McMurdo Sound. She was not large enough to transport all the men and stores, but, as part of the I.G.Y. programme, the Americans were also establishing a station in McMurdo Sound, and kindly offered shipping space to take the excess.

By the middle of December the *Endeavour* had finished loading and left Wellington for Christchurch. The Duke of Edinburgh was spending a short time there in the Royal Yacht *Britannia* before leaving to visit the British Antarctic Bases in Graham Land. He inspected *Endeavour* and later entertained the members of the Expedition on board *Britannia*. On 21st December the New Zealand people gave them a tremendous send-off, and escorted by the frigates *Pukaki* and *Hawea*, the *Endeavour* plunged steadily into the Southern Ocean and the adventures ahead.

It was bright and sunny on Christmas Day as they all gathered on the foc'sle where Captain Kirkwood conducted the Christmas Service. Already they were sighting large numbers of whales and the air was full of birds, but on Boxing Day they ran into fog and had to reduce speed in an area of icebergs. By the 27th they had entered light pack ice and as this began to thicken the two escorting frigates decided it was time to turn back. Exchanging shouts and cheers, to the accompaniment of a succession of toots and wails from their sirens, *Pukaki* and *Hawea* withdrew to warmer waters, leaving *Endeavour* to plough steadily southwards. By the 29th pack ice covered almost the whole sea, leaving only small leads of open water. When the floes closed together the ship was hove-to, waiting for the leads to open up under the influence of changing winds and current. Often the ice was soft and rotten and could be broken up by the ship's repeated onslaught. Birds, seals and whales were everywhere visible among the ice floes and soon everyone was enjoying the antics of the absurd little Adélie penguins.

By New Year's Eve they had broken through the worst of the pack, but a strong southerly gale had arisen and by midnight *Endeavour* was wallowing through huge waves, being severely buffeted by heavy ice floes that it was impossible to dodge. As she passed through the last belt of ice, its damping effect on the waves was removed and they entered the open water of the Ross Sea into the teeth of a southerly storm. Huge waves, a black lowering sky and frequent snow showers seemed to close around the violently tossing little vessel, sending most members of the Expedition green-faced to their bunks. Around noon on New Year's Day the storm reached a crescendo of fury and the party were seriously concerned for the dogs and the vehicles stowed on the forward deck. To limit the amount of water sweeping over the decks Captain Kirkwood was just maintaining steering way, but one great wave crashed over the bows demolishing several kennels, and to extricate the dogs from the debris and tether them at the stern of the ship was an exciting, and on the heaving deck, dangerous operation. The dogs had got thoroughly wet, never a good thing for huskies, but they seemed none the worse for their adventure.

Two days later the weather improved considerably and early

in the afternoon the bridge reported 'Land ahead'. Everyone rushed up with binoculars, eager to pick out the volcanic cones of Mount Erebus and Mount Terror, the former with its characteristic plume of smoke and steam—but they were still almost a hundred miles away. By late afternoon the Western Mountains of Victoria Land appeared to starboard as they approached the entrance to McMurdo Sound. Then, to their disgust, they ran into more heavy pack ice and spent the night immobilized in its grip.

Time was now becoming very important and as the U.S.S. *Glacier*, the most powerful ice-breaker in the world, was operating in the vicinity, Captain Kirkwood asked for its assistance. In an impressive exhibition of power she steamed towards them, quite unconcerned by the heavy pack and throwing great blocks of ice aside in all directions. The *Endeavour* thankfully followed her lead into the open water of McMurdo Sound and was soon anchored to the edge of the sea ice opposite Butter Point.

Unloading began immediately. First off were the dogs, which were tethered in a long line, leaping and cavorting in their delight at being back on snow once more. Soon they were followed by tractors, sledges, tents, food, and all the equipment for the first inland ground reconnaissance which would enable Ed Hillary to decide on the best site for the base, for at this time nine miles of sea ice separated the ship from the actual coast.

The intention was to use the Ferrar Glacier as a highway to the polar plateau, for Scott had been that way in 1902. Soon after midnight on the morning of 7th January the reconnaissance party set off with dog teams. They soon found that there was no route up the Ferrar which vehicles could follow—indeed the lower glacier was impassable even for dog sledges because of the bare windswept ice and the summer thaw streams which had cut up the surface. The Royal New Zealand Air Force contingent had been working busily uncrating the fuselage of the Beaver and fitting the wings to make the plane operational. As soon as this was finished Ed himself flew up the length of the glacier and confirmed the findings of the reconnaissance party. This was a serious setback because a route up to the plateau was essential to enable the Ross Sea Party to lay the depots, and for the Crossing Party to descend at the end of their journey.

Meanwhile a tractor reconnaissance party was seeking an area where the five hundred tons of stores could be hauled up and a suitable site found for Scott Base. Butter Point proved an unsatisfactory proposition, but, after examination, Pram Point on Ross Island seemed to offer an ideal position. There was ample room on several broad rock terraces for the various huts, with space for an airstrip within a few hundred yards. It was a nine-mile haul from the ship, and as the Americans were at the same time consolidating and storing their I.G.Y. base at Hut Point, only two miles distant, using the same tracks across the sea ice for their heavy tractors and sledges, the first part of the route was in a frightful condition. Great holes had been churned in the surface of the ice, which had then filled with water; it took the New Zealanders a long time to find a way among them and sometimes they had to drive straight through, which involved a frightening descent into several feet of water and some rapid mental calculations as to the depth of sea ice left between the tractor and several hundred fathoms of cold sea water. But when finally this area was crossed, the tractors came on to soft snow and the party were able to find a satisfactory route around Cape Armitage.

Work began at once, and throughout the twenty-four hours the tractors wound their way from the ship to the site, bringing in the stores, while the six huts took shape and the wireless masts were erected.

Meanwhile the field party were now searching for an alternative route up to the plateau. Ed's thoughts had turned to the Skelton Glacier and on 18th January Bill Cranfield flew him south between Black and White Islands and around the tip of Minna Bluff where the pressure ridges and crevasses were very bad indeed. They then flew west into the mouth of the Skelton and found the lower trunk of the glacier heavily crevassed at the sides, but with a relatively unbroken stretch running up the centre. As they flew up the steep middle section, they became more and more optimistic, for although there were large areas of crevasses, it appeared from the air at least that by following rather a winding route, vehicles would be able to dodge most of them. Presently, at nearly seven thousand feet, they saw the great snow field *névé* which fed the glacier, and in the distance

---

Névé is old snow which has been transformed into denser material.

could see a rock wall which they thought to be the edge of the plateau itself. A second flight with John Claydon as pilot completed the examination of the route. This time they flew direct to the névé and then on towards a gap in the surrounding mountain wall. The névé extended upwards in a wide gradual slope through the mountains and finally merged into the vast open expanse of the polar plateau—it was certainly a most promising route.

The summer was passing and there was no time to waste if they were to carry out a ground reconnaissance that season. On 25th January Richard Brooke, Murray Ellis, Harry Ayres and Murray Douglas were flown to the foot of the Skelton Glacier where they established the Skelton Depot and then set out to find a vehicle route up to the plateau. They had two dog teams, sledges, food and camping equipment, and started up the glacier next morning. This was also an auspicious day back at Scott Base, for the unloading of the *Endeavour* was completed and those at the base could now focus their whole attention on the buildings and the internal fittings. Covered ways were also built between the six huts for protection against the weather, for during the winter the base would become buried in snow and it would be convenient to be able to move from one building to the other without going outside. Unlike Shackleton, Scott Base could be built on rock, and so each year would reappear as the drifted snow melted and ran down to the sea.

It was 180 miles across the Ross Ice Shelf from Scott Base to the Skelton Depot and Bob Miller and Ron Carlyon set off with a dog team to establish the route. Neither of these men had run dogs by themselves before, but they had learnt quickly on the Tasman Glacier in New Zealand and were now able to maintain an average speed of sixteen miles a day. From the depot they went on to map the lower reaches of the glacier. (See map, page 186.)

Meanwhile the Beaver had been flying in load after load of food and fuel to stock the Skelton Depot for the Crossing Party's arrival the next season. The two geologists, Bernie Gunn and Guy Warren, went on one of these flights and were set down with a light Fibreglass sledge to do geological work up and down the Skelton. They crossed the heavily crevassed edges of the glacier and visited every major rock bluff, examining the rocks and taking geological specimens. They ended by climbing Mount

Harmsworth, a peak of 9,090 feet, from a camp on the low glacier floor—a marathon effort of twenty-three hours up and down.

The Skelton reconnaissance party under Richard Brooke had meanwhile been making steady progress. Soft snow in the steep middle section had slowed them up considerably and they had been forced to 'relay' their loads, taking part of the load forward and then returning for the remainder, thereby having to travel at least three times the distance of each forward move. Their route through the crevassed areas wound unevenly from side to side, but once they reached the névé the going was much more straightforward and in two days they reached the long slope that breaks through the mountains to the plateau. Here the surface was rough and hard and they suffered from the constant wind and the cold temperatures, but they pushed on over the edge to reach the polar plateau at over eight thousand feet on 8th February. On this day also the Beaver completed the stocking of the Skelton Depot with seven tons of food and fuel.

With these two tasks completed, the next morning was to be a critical one, for it was planned to make the first aircraft landings on the polar plateau. To establish the necessary depots for the Crossing Party on the plateau, they intended to use the aircraft, which would be received at the selected sites by the ground parties. But although the landing of the loaded aircraft could easily be accomplished, it was not known whether they would be able to take off again because of the thinner air at over eight thousand feet. Particular concern was felt about the Auster, which had so much less power than the Beaver.

Under a clear sky and in bright sunlight, both aircraft took off from Scott Base and headed for the Skelton, Ed Hillary flying in the Beaver with John Claydon. They climbed steadily over the jagged ribs of the Western Mountains, sidled over the steep glaciers draining off Mount Huggins and emerged over the Skelton Névé. Still climbing they crossed the last wall under Mount Feather and began to search the plateau for the tents of the dog party. Seeing small black specks in the vast white 'snow desert' away to the east, John Claydon circled several times before he found a suitable place to bring the plane in to land. The temperature was −27°F with a strong wind, and as John and Ed climbed out to greet Richard Brooke's party, the wind-burned and bearded faces of the sledgers plainly showed the effects of the rigorous weather. It was agreed that the dog party would remain on the plateau while the Beaver stocked 'Plateau Depot'. John and Ed them climbed back into the plane for the critical moment of take-off.

This was the crucial test—getting the plane off the ground again in the thin air. They taxied away to the take-off point and then John gave her full throttle. To start with their progress seemed painfully slow, but gradually the Beaver gathered speed and, to their great relief, leapt into the air without apparent difficulty. The Auster had been standing watch overhead, but as soon as the Beaver was safely airborne, Bill Cranfield brought it down to a smooth landing. At this altitude it was at its limit of power, and from high above Ed and John watched anxiously as it attempted to take off again. It seemed to go on and on across the snow, gaining no speed at all, but finally it staggered into the air and circled to join them. Delighted to have proved that in an emergency the Auster could be used for landings on the plateau, they all returned to base to prepare the airlift of supplies to Plateau Depot. By flying twenty-four hours a day whenever weather permitted the airmen stocked the depot despite temperatures in the minus thirties and persistent winds of twenty knots or more. Meanwhile Richard Brooke's dog party retreated to the upper reaches of the Skelton Glacier, where they remained surveying until the end of the month. There, some two thousand feet below the plateau, the temperatures were from ten to fifteen degrees warmer.

All the outside work at Scott Base had now been finished—the huts were firmly tied to the ground with steel wire ropes; the covered ways between them were finished and were already being used to store foodstuffs on packing-case shelves; the nine radio masts—two of them eighty feet high and seven sixty feet high— made a most impressive array. Already they had two radio schedules a day with New Zealand and had despatched their first photograph by radio. Early on the morning of 22nd February the *Endeavour* sailed for home, leaving them in a strong position to face the winter.

With the departure of the ship they experienced a period of

dull grey weather; temperatures fell and heavy cloud dimmed the rapidly shortening days. At the end of the month, in one clear flying day, several airlifts evacuated all the men and dogs who had been sitting out the storms at the Skelton Depot. For the first time the wintering party were all together at base and it was possible to institute a regular routine of duties.

Early in March, during a period of clear weather, the Beaver was used for a number of long reconnaissance flights with a view to gaining more knowledge for the party's spring activities. They flew several hundred miles south of Plateau Depot, exploring the route they hoped to follow towards the Pole next season. In addition, several flights were made to the north along the mountains of Victoria Land. These showed great snow-free valleys, large lakes (frozen at this time of year), and even extensive river systems which excited their interest in this area. Soon they were planning to send surveyors and geologists into it during the following season.

Although it was never part of the official plan, Ed had always hoped that it would be possible to use the Ferguson tractors as well as dogs on the depot-laying journey towards the Pole. To this end various modifications had already been made by the engineers, Jim Bates and Murray Ellis. Ed now decided to test the vehicles by driving along the route covered on foot by Wilson, Bowers and Cherry-Garrard in their amazing 'Worst Journey in the World', in 1911. This entailed crossing the Ross Ice Shelf from Scott Base to Cape Crozier at the eastern tip of Ross Island—a round trip of about a hundred miles.

On 19th March Ed himself, with Murray Ellis, Jim Bates and Peter Mulgrew, left the base with two tractors and four laden sledges. In bad visibility and deep, soft snow they fumbled their way through the pressure ridges and crevasses, then across the Windless Bight in the shadow of Mount Erebus. At first their progress was very slow; it took two days to cover twenty-five miles, but as they went they carried out various experiments with the sledges and repaired and modified the track mechanism of the Fergusons which improved their performance. On the third day they reached firm surfaces and were able to race round Cape Mackay and along the trough between the walls of Mount Terror and the broken pressure ice of the Ross Ice Shelf. In the dim evening light they scratched their way up a long icy slope to a snowy shelf at the foot of the 'Knoll' which crowns Cape Crozier and established a camp which they occupied for several days in continuously windy weather. It was very cold with drifting snow.

Here they found the remains of the stone hut built by Wilson's party. Like a monument above it was the upright framework of a manhauling sledge chafed by nearly half a century of wind and drift, but still in excellent condition. Digging the ice out of the hut they uncovered many interesting relics—some of Dr. Wilson's drawing pencils, test tubes, thermometers, unexposed film, a blubber stove, a heavy pick-axe, and skins and blubber from Emperor penguins.

On 24th March they set off for home, first of all digging away the piles of snow which had accumulated round the tents and tractors. Making a cautious descent down the ice slope into the trough, they made good speed back to Cape Mackay, but the temperature was steadily falling, and in the darkness as they struggled across the soft snow of the Windless Bight the thermometers were showing −46°F.

The lights on one of the tractors failed, and those on the other proved temperamental as the cold affected the batteries, while ground fog came up as they approached Pram Point, and ice developed in a carburettor and a frozen fuel line. Finding a way through the pressure ridges near Scott Base was a long business, and it was a tired party that drove into the base, having covered 47½ miles in fourteen hours. But they were greatly encouraged by the performance of their vehicles and determined to work on them during the winter with a view to taking them south with the dog teams in the spring.

The sun finally left them on 14th April but there was one more journey planned before the winter set in in earnest. This was a pilgrimage to Captain Scott's old hut at Cape Evans. It proved to be a large-scale operation. Murray Ellis and Peter Mulgrew manhauled their way across, towing their camping gear behind them; the two pilots, John Claydon and Bill Cranfield, did the same, but took advantage of the opportunity to use and test their special air emergency rations and the emergency tent and equipment they always carried in the aircraft; eight others trekked across with four dog teams.

79

Their arrival was a great disappointment. The ground around the hut was covered with rubbish, empty tins and the carcases of seals, frozen since 1910, strewn in every direction. The bottom floor of the hut was filled with ice and only the top floor was accessible. This room was an unpleasant mixture of disorder and dirt and obviously little attempt had been made by the various parties who had wintered there since Scott's expedition to keep the hut tidy. It seemed a poor memorial to a great man and they were glad to leave. The situation is different now, for in January 1958 Captain Kirkwood and the crew of the *Endeavour* spent some time at Cape Evans, cleaning out the hut and getting rid of the rubbish.

The Ross Sea Party had finished a season of much useful work. It was good to know that they had found a satisfactory route to the polar plateau and that already two fully stocked depots had been established for the Crossing Party. They now faced the winter with confidence, and looked forward with impatience for the return of the sun and the renewal of their field activities.

Geological camp in the Shackleton Range

Taffy Williams with dog team in the Shackleton Range

Evening in the Shackleton Range

North-west end of the Shackleton Range. The Air Camp was near the moraine in the middle distance

Moraine near the Air Camp at the north-west end of the Shackleton Range

Vehicles passing the western end of the Shackleton Range towards Recovery Glacier

Sno-Cat 'Rock 'n Roll's'
first crevasse

Junction of the Mill and Beardmore Glaciers, seen during the Trans-polar flight

7. The second winter

Our three bases were now established and by the end of March flying would have to cease. We would all settle down to our scientific work during the four months of darkness and to planning and preparing for our spring journeys which, we hoped, would culminate in the successful crossing of the continent.

At Shackleton two radio schedules were kept each day with Hal, Jon and Ken, wintering at South Ice, and every Monday we contacted the New Zealanders at Scott Base. When conditions were good enough it was possible to talk to them freely by radio telephone, but if there were atmospheric disturbances we had to fall back on sending messages in morse.

Hal at South Ice was fond of making up poetry or short songs and many of these he would read to us over the air. On birthdays or party nights the radio exchanges between Shackleton and South Ice were often hilarious. Once we were told by our American friends at a neighbouring station that our frequency, 6684 kilocycles, was 'Quite the best programme on the air!' It appeared that they had taken to monitoring our transmissions.

Our first task was to make sure that our aircraft were adequately protected for the winter. Peter Weston removed the tall rudder from the tail of the Otter, then prepared the engine against the winter and sealed every door and window against drift. A wide, shelving pit was dug to a depth of about four feet and a tractor towed the plane into this so that the skis and undercarriage stood in the deepest part, while the wings lay horizontal and low to the surface. Peter built sloping timber wind-breaks behind the trailing edges of the wings and tailplane, and a strong fence of steel wire mesh in front of the aircraft reduced the direct force of the southerly winds. The lower edge of the

fence was two feet above the snow, so that the wind could scour the surface beneath and thus prevent the formation of snow-drifts.

At Scott Base they removed the wings of their Beaver and stowed them in a crate. The fuselage was then towed to an exposed position to prevent the accumulation of drift and care-fully tied down. In this way, with the engine muffled and all nooks and crannies sealed against drift, the plane was safe until the spring.

The two Austers, being very much smaller, did not require so much attention. The size of the ailerons, elevators and rudder made it possible for us at Shackleton to lock them with wooden clamps, and the plane was so light that we could easily move it to face into the wind. At Scott Base they decided to keep their Auster operational throughout the winter and it was left on the airfield behind a wind-break of wire netting. Each month when the moon rose there would be signs of great activity on the Scott Base airstrip, the twinkle of lights and the roar of hot-air blowers. After removing the large quantities of fine drift snow that, despite the sealing, forced their way inside the wings and the fuselage, and warming the frozen engine, a few lamps were spread down the runway, and the little aircraft would roar off into the moonlit sky for a short trip around McMurdo Sound.

We were concerned for our dogs. At Scott Base, where there were sixty, they were able to live outside all through the winter and, again when the moon came up each month, they were harnessed to their sledges and given a run. Racing over the rough sea ice was an exhilarating experience for both dogs and men as it was impossible to pick out obstacles in the moonlight—for the driver the only thing to do was to cling to the sledge and hope for the best.

At Shackleton, as the winds rose and the temperatures fell, they lay curled up on the snow above our buried hut, with only their fur and blubber to protect them. As the wind continually swept the snow from the hard compacted surface, they were even denied the usual protection of accumulating drift to keep them warm. Sometimes when we went to visit them they would rise to greet us, but often their warmth had melted the snow, which had then frozen again and tore the hair from their bodies as they struggled to their feet.

We decided to dig new tunnels for their protection and determined that there must be plenty of headroom as well as space to saw up the seal meat under shelter. Making a tunnel 140 feet long by 8 feet deep and 4 feet wide, we cut alcoves in the walls on alternate sides to prevent the dogs reaching each other at the ends of their chains. Later on, the main power system provided the tunnel with electricity for twelve hours each day, and the dogs lived in considerable comfort and relative warmth—for even with an outdoor temperature of $-60°F$, the heat from their bodies kept the tunnel just above zero.

One of the least popular chores was cutting up the seal meat. The carcase had first to be dug out from the snow and then cut into pieces by two men using a great cross-cut saw. These were then split up with an axe or sawn into 'logs' weighing four to six pounds. One such 'log' was fed to each dog every other day.

All the bases were carrying out scientific work. At South Ice a Dexion lattice mast was erected which soon became festooned with recording instruments, including anemometers and thermometers every few feet right down to the surface. These provided Hal Lister with wind and temperature records for his glaciological work. At the top of the mast was a small red light which could be switched on from inside the hut to call an absorbed scientist in when lunch was ready.

Jon Stephenson was studying ice crystals, and to obtain the specimens he dug a pit fifty feet deep from inside one of the snow tunnels. From this depth he bored a hole for another hundred feet down, bringing up a core of ice in sections eighteen inches long. By studying the snow strata both in the walls of the pit and in the cores, much was learnt about the annual snow fall for centuries past. In fact, the snow recovered from the deepest point fell at the time of the Battle of Agincourt!

At Shackleton Allan Rogers had some complicated instruments called Integrating Motor Pneumotachographs (known as 'IMPS' for short), with which he could measure and study the energy expended by a man both at work and at rest—provided, of course, that he could persuade any of us to put up with the discomfort of wearing a mask over his face and a pack on his back while going about his normal work. Soon, members of the party could be seen cooking or sweeping, hauling sledges or building, while wearing IMPS.

Geoffrey Pratt very helpfully undertook to wear the instrument day and night (except at meals) for a whole week. He found it an irksome and uncomfortable experience and even suffered from frostbite on his face through wearing the mask long hours out of doors, in temperatures below $-50°F$. However, in the end it was poor Allan who had the worst of it, because he had to follow Geoffrey about all day to see that the IMP was working, and so had to help his energetic subject with all kinds of tasks which were certainly nothing to do with a doctor. Then at mealtimes Allan had to weigh all the food that Geoffrey ate besides questioning the cook to find out what had gone into making the various dishes. This was necessary so that the energy consumed by Geoffrey in the form of food could be compared with energy he expended. So it was that mealtimes passed with Geoffrey eating heartily and poor Allan still hard at work in the kitchen, with often the prospect of little left for him to eat!

After one sleepless night due to the gurgling noises made by Geoffrey and the IMP while he slept, we banished him from the bunk-room to the attic. Still there was no rest for Allan, for he had to follow him and even remain awake to see that the mask was not displaced by his 'guinea-pig' while he slept. At the end of the week it was the doctor who was exhausted!

An outdoor task undertaken by David Pratt was the measurement of friction between different types of sledge-runner materials in varying temperatures and on different types of snow surfaces. He used small manhauled sledges carrying a known load, the amount of effort required to keep the sledge in movement being measured electrically by strain gauges. He was constantly looking for unsuspecting people to act as hauliers. I was lucky to do my stint of forty hauls in good conditions, with the temperature at only − 19°F, but a few days later Allan Rogers found himself doing the same thing in − 60°F. Suddenly he realized that he could make use of the same activity for his IMP work and, in no time at all, the unfortunate Taffy Williams found himself torn from his nice warm radio-room, wearing an IMP and manhauling a sledge in the outer darkness. As he stumbled from one invisible snowdrift to another, Allan and David each cried his own directions, until the protesting Taffy was at last discharged from duty (exhausted), and another victim found.

We also wanted to measure the tides. At Scott Base a gauge was mounted in a hole cut in the bay ice just below the site, but its operation was constantly threatened by the ice movement, and the increasing depth of ice that formed on the surface of the Sound eventually made it useless.

Simply explained, the usual way of measuring the tide is to record the level of the sea as it moves up and down a pillar fixed to the solid ground. This could not be done at Shackleton because we lacked the most important part of the apparatus—solid ground! Everything for miles around was afloat and itself rose and fell with the sea. Geoffrey Pratt decided that a delicate instrument called a gravimeter would be sensitive enough to measure this movement, and digging a pit twenty feet deep a few hundred yards from the base, he constructed a complicated piece of apparatus which switched itself on automatically for ten minutes every hour, during which time a series of photographs was taken of the gravimeter reading, while a light flashed on a pole above the surface to warn off vehicle drivers and heavy-footed pedestrians. Indoors, flashing lights also showed that the apparatus was working, but to us the particular magic of Geoffrey's instrument was its ability to call for his help if anything went wrong by switching on and off the bunk light over his bed. As a result of these observations we learnt that the 1,300-foot thick ice shelf on which Shackleton was built rose and fell as much as eleven feet with the tide.

The sun left us on 23rd April, but inside our huts we were always busy. At Shackleton each man was duty cook for four days at a time, helped by two 'gashmen' who were responsible for bringing in the snow to be melted for our water supply, keeping the stoves supplied with fuel, washing up, keeping the hut tidy, and—perhaps the worst chore of all—disposing of the rubbish. This entailed carrying a twelve-gallon bucket of kitchen waste up a flight of snow steps to the surface where, more often than not, the wind would whip the contents over the gashmen as they staggered away into the drift.

After a time we could bear this no longer, so we dug out an extension tunnel from the bottom of the snow steps, and made a deep waste-pit in an unusual manner. First we made a small hole about eighteen inches deep in the snow. Into this we poured a pint of petrol which soaked in immediately. Taking care that there were no small pools of petrol on the surface, a match was applied, and the petrol burnt slowly, gradually melting a cavity. Each time the flames went out more petrol was poured into the deepening hole and set alight, and in two hours, with the use of four gallons of petrol, we had a pit twenty-four feet deep. This served us excellently as a waste-pit until the base was abandoned in November.

After a few weeks we noticed that when a bucket of water had been tipped into this waste-pit, there was a pause followed by a distant rumbling gurgle. Then we found that cold air was rising from the pit, and we realized that the bottom of the pit had broken through into a crevasse which ran almost under the base hut.

At Scott Base they had a full-time cook, helped by two duty 'gashmen' who were on for a week at a time. On Sundays the cook was given a complete rest and the gashmen prepared the meals, which led to keen competition for original menus.

Many firms had given us labour-saving equipment which greatly added to our comfort at base. Both at Scott and at Shackleton the Singer sewing machines were never idle as we made hundreds of trail flags and mended or modified clothing and tents. During the winter, sledges were stripped down and repaired, dog traces spliced and new dog harnesses made. As there were thirteen of us sharing the hut at Shackleton, each man had the bathroom in turn for a day at a time. At the same time he did his personal laundry with the Hoover washing machine which we had been given.

Installing our bathroom had presented us with some unexpected problems. When an Antarctic hut is built on rock, as at Scott Base, it is very unwise to allow the bathwater to run away through the normal waste-plug as it will freeze on the rock below, gradually building up ice beneath the floor and very soon preventing any further escape. We had therefore expected to bale out our bathwater and empty it outside, but finding our hut at Shackleton built on a great depth of snow, we now thought that it would accept the bath waste—as indeed it did. Unfortunately the bath supplied to us had no waste-plug!

David Stratton told us he had discovered that this type of bath was made specially for sale in Aden, as Arabs apparently did not require waste-pipes. But why not? We spent a great deal of time inventing stories of a long camel caravan winding over the hot sands of Arabia, each camel bearing two white enamelled cast-iron baths like panniers on either side of its swaying humps. But what on earth did the Arabs do with the waste water when the baths were finally in use?

We never did find out, but our engineers decided to try to make a hole in the normal place in the bath and to drain the waste water away beneath the hut. This was not an easy task without chipping the enamel or cracking the iron, and during their initial experiments in devising a suitable plug for the hole, the bather was frequently left sitting in the empty bath, high, dry, soapy, and unamused.

Up at South Ice the weather was nearly always more severe than at Shackleton, for not only was the station farther south and away from the sea, but it stood at a much greater altitude. (As we could seldom boast the low temperatures they recorded,

Shackleton came to be known scornfully to the South Ice party as 'The Banana Belt'.) It was quite difficult for only three men to carry out all the scientific work they had undertaken as well as the normal chores of cooking, bringing in fuel and ice, keeping radio schedules and looking after generators and other equipment.

At Scott Base daily classes in morse and polar navigation were instituted to prepare the members of the field parties for the work ahead. Every morning the mess hut was filled with a band of beginners straining their ears to receive the immaculate morse of their instructor, Ted Gawn. The first few months were the worst, but after that everyone became reasonably proficient and by the end of the winter they could all send and receive messages at between six and twelve words a minute.

Bob Miller was responsible for navigation classes and the two geologists, Bernie Gunn and Guy Warren, gave a series of lectures designed to give the members of the field parties sufficient knowledge to enable them to make an intelligent collection of rock specimens for later examination by experts.

One of the busiest places at each base was the garage workshop. Here the engineers worked long hours preparing and modifying the vehicles for the testing time ahead of them. At Scott Base the original plan was for the depots towards the Pole to be established by dog teams and for the supplies to be flown in by air. But Ed Hillary had been very impressed with the performance of his small Ferguson tractors and finally decided to use these also for the southern journey. It was a large-scale operation preparing them. Over the driver's seat was welded a powerful crash bar to give some protection should the vehicle go down a crevasse or roll over. Around this a cab, or rather a wind-break, was constructed from canvas to keep out a little of the Antarctic wind. The track system was strengthened and an enormous amount of work was done on the tracks themselves to try and improve their grip in soft snow. The motors were overhauled, the electrical wiring system simplified, and any unnecessary parts of the body were cut away to save weight. A light, portable garage was constructed out of canvas, with a collapsible framework of three-quarter-inch piping, in case of a major breakdown; a strong tow-bar was welded to the front of each vehicle, and sixty-foot lengths of Terylene towrope, with an eight-ton breaking strain, were cut and spliced.

At Shackleton David and Roy worked on the vehicles one after the other, stripping down tracks, welding on recovery equipment for use should they fall into crevasses, and overhauling all the engines. The days were not long enough for everything that had to be done.

As a relaxation our engineers had made a large fish trap out of wire netting which they had lowered through a hole cut in the sea ice, although as the water was three thousand feet deep, there was no hope of bottom fishing. One evening George Lowe and I went down with them to visit this trap. Leaving Shackleton in a brisk wind and heavy snow, we found it difficult to find our way along the two-mile route in the dark, but, helped by the marker stakes and stretches of the old track which had not been drifted over, we reached the edge of the sea ice. The hole through which the trap had been let down was frozen over and when we broke through, countless clusters of ice crystals an inch or more in diameter floated to the surface. When at last we obtained a patch of clear water, we could see hundreds of pink, shrimp-like creatures in the light of our torches. These were *euphausea*, or krill, the main food of many species of whale, and this was all that the trap contained. Not intending to return empty-handed, we collected as many of them as we could, thinking they would make a surprise dish for David Stratton's birthday the next day.

Suddenly there was a swirl of water and a seal surfaced to breathe, but he was as startled as we were and disappeared in an instant. As we turned back towards the Shackleton beacon light shining through the driving snow, it occurred to me that people at home might think us slightly mad to go shrimping in a snow-storm at dead of night in the Antarctic winter—but to us it was a relaxation to leave base and do something different from the daily routine.

Our special dish of sea-food was duly prepared in honour of David's birthday and looked most attractive. We all gathered round as manfully he tackled the delicate pink pile, only to find that each multi-legged corpse contained no more than a few drops of pink oil!

By 18th June the spirit of Midwinter was with us and most of
our indoor activities were directed towards preparing for the
great day. Our living-room was hung with paper chains and
clusters of coloured balloons; David Stratton was finishing the
lettering of the menu cards, while George Lowe printed the
photographs which would be stuck into them; Ralph Lenton was
turning out a succession of cakes, pastries, sausage rolls and cocktail snacks, while David Pratt and Roy Homard refused us entrance to the engineering workshop where we were invited to a
special party on Midwinter morning. Gordon Haslop had for some
time been busy with mysterious preparations of his own, which

90

included digging several trenches and creeping furtively round the site clutching various flares, explosives, Very pistols and detonators.

From our meat store, a snow pit not far from the hut, we brought in a trussed turkey, a large joint of pork, half a side of bacon which had been saved for the occasion, and several pounds of fresh potatoes. These had frozen so hard that they rattled in the sack like stones, and indeed looked like pebbles from a beach. We found that as long as they were kept frozen and then suddenly thawed by cooking, they remained in excellent condition.

The same kind of preparations were going on at Scott Base and in a more modest way at South Ice. Our different radio schedules brought us messages of greeting from all over the world, including a topical Antarctic pantomime specially written for us by those at our London headquarters. On Midwinter's Eve we enjoyed a two-way radio conversation with our other half at Scott Base. Greetings were exchanged and after some hilarious confusion as to Zone Time, Local Time, Greenwich Mean Time and public-house opening time, it was firmly established that they had stolen a march on us and had already started their celebrations.

On 21st June—Midwinter Day—we rose late for breakfast, and then everybody helped with the normal chores of sweeping, cleaning and bringing in ice and coal, before dressing to go to the Pratt–Homard cocktail party—although it was darkly rumoured by the non-engineers that the 'cocktails' would consist mainly of petrol, flavoured with grease and oil! We set out for the workshop fully clothed in windproofs and gloves, expecting to stumble over the intervening snowdrifts, but to our surprise the snow reflected the flickering light of dozens of paraffin flares marking the two-hundred-yard route.

Inside the workshop it was beautifully warm, for the small coal fire in the annexe was roaring and the temperature of the whole building had been raised to $+ 35°F$. We were able to strip off our outdoor clothing and stand about in comfort admiring the new photographs and coloured posters which decorated the walls. The shouts of welcome which greeted each new arrival and the general air of gaiety was enhanced by a background of Irish jigs from the record-player, and soon someone thought of fixing a large

meteorological balloon to the exhaust of a Weasel and starting
the engine. Slowly at first, but with increasing speed, it grew to
gigantic proportions before exploding with a satisfying bang!

This entertainment was followed by the explanation of Gordon
Haslop's strange behaviour during the previous few days. The
'Haslop Firework Display' began with a series of detonations
spelling 'T.A.E.' in morse and continued with flares and rockets,
while the flitting figure of Gordon could be seen silhouetted
against the lights, clearly clutching a beer mug in one hand while
setting off fireworks with the other. It was a fine show.

South Ice came through on the radio to exchange greetings and tell us about the roast beef lunch they had just finished and how they were already looking forward to chicken for dinner. At 3.30 p.m. we sat down to a splendid meal which included green turtle soup, roast turkey, plum pudding and ice cream. The table was decorated with crackers and presents and in due course most of us were wearing paper hats and playing musical instruments.

Later that evening, after a suitable pause for digestion and recovery, we enjoyed a buffet supper, which included even mustard and cress sandwiches (grown in boxes in the loft of the hut), the first fresh vegetable we had tasted since the *Magga Dan* left us. Ralph Lenton felt inspired to entertain us with a wonderful version of the Dance of the Seven Veils, while an improvised band—I imagine the first Antarctic Skiffle Group—played vigorously on any available article.

Such was our Midwinter, and after it we settled down to the second half of the long dark night, always looking forward to the return of the sun in August. We went back to our regular routine of tending our instruments, looking after the dogs, working on the vehicles, digging out buried sledges and the thousand other things which made the time of preparation for spring all too short. We worked hard on the camping equipment, mending tents, binding tent poles with tape or balloon cord to strengthen them, checking and repacking ration boxes, overhauling field radio equipment—all laborious jobs which took many hours.

By the end of July the temperature at Shackleton dropped to − 64°F with a twenty-five knot wind. At South Ice it was − 71°F. But by the beginning of August both bases enjoyed the faint glow of the returning sun reflected from below the horizon. Day by day the light on the clouds became more colourful and steadily increased until it was possible for us to move about outside without the aid of lanterns to light our way.

Then on 14th August, four days before it was due, the sun topped the horizon and Peter Weston came running into the hut to report its appearance. Several of us rushed outside wearing only indoor clothes to see a red glow on the northern horizon—then the wind and a temperature of − 56°F drove us back inside again. During the next quarter of an hour the upper rim of the sun appeared to rise and set several times, owing to the effect of the refraction of the light. Indeed it was only due to this refraction by the atmosphere that we saw the sun four days before it was due to show above the horizon.

At Scott Base they had to wait longer for the sun as its appearance was cut off by the bulk of Observation Hill. It was not until 23rd August that Bill Cranfield, flying in the Auster, saw it from high over McMurdo Sound. It was an exciting moment and gave a lift to all their spirits, for they were all impatient to get into the field.

Both parties planned to start the spring journeys early in September, and by the middle of August we at Shackleton began digging out the Otter from the deep pit in which it had spent the winter. In spite of the return of the sun it was bitterly cold. Temperatures were still down to — 67°F and we had to choose the better weather periods to clear away the large drifts which had formed around the plane. It was then hauled to the surface by a Sno-Cat and drawn to a level place near the aircraft workshop where it could be de-iced and prepared for flying. It was so cold throughout this operation that shovelling snow was a much more attractive occupation than handling the towropes and shackles with freezing fingers.

To enable Peter Weston to get the Auster ready for the season's flying, we put up a tent over the engine; inside this he could work regardless of the weather conditions. The rest of us were busy digging out sledges which had been drifted over, making up steel wire and Terylene safety ropes for the vehicles, mending tents, making dog harnesses, digging up stores to last until our departure in November, and, most important of all, training the dogs after their long period underground.

For the first two weeks of September we experienced blizzard conditions and any sort of travelling was out of the question. Then suddenly, on the 17th, we received bad news from Halley Bay. Robin Smart, the leader and medical officer of the Royal Society Expedition, had fallen down and injured himself internally, and his condition was causing anxiety. The Auster was almost ready to fly, so I decided to send Allan Rogers to the Royal Society base at the first break in the weather. Two days later conditions had improved sufficiently for a test flight, and on the 20th he took off with Gordon Haslop piloting, to make the two-and-a-half hours' flight.

Five hours later I returned from a dog training run to hear John Lewis talking to the plane over the radio. Gordon was still in the air; it was getting dark and he had missed the coloured lights put out for his guidance at Halley Bay. He now had only enough fuel in his tank for one hour's flying and had decided to land while there was still sufficient light. We believed he had overshot the base, so told him to come down as close as possible to the edge of the ice shelf—thus if a search became necessary we would only have to follow the coast to find him. We heard him land safely and before he closed down his radio to conserve his batteries he acknowledged our message telling him that we would keep radio watch every day from eight o'clock each morning.

Gordon and Allan were wearing thick, down clothing, and had with them single, light-weight sleeping bags, R.A.F. 'survival rations' for three weeks and enough paraffin to have a 'brew-up' or hot drink first thing in the morning and last thing at night.

Having landed the plane when it was almost dark, their first need was shelter, so they began to dig in the snow, using a sheath knife and their hands. At the end of six hours their hole was, as Gordon later told us, 'about the size of a two-man coffin'. They roofed over the top with the engine cover from the aircraft and settled down to a cramped and uncomfortable night, shivering a good deal and sleeping only in short snatches, ready to be picked up the next day.

But the weather then clamped down again, with high winds and constant drift, and for eleven days flying was out of the question. Each day they gradually enlarged their hole until they could stand up in comfort. By the end of a week there was a ledge down each side on which they slept, another across one end on which the Primus stood, and shelves and niches in the walls for their belongings.

As the blizzards continued, the aircraft had constantly to be dug free of snowdrifts and kept facing into the wind, and to help the search party we were preparing to fly off at the first opportunity, they marked out a runway with slabs of ice and fluorescent dye. The survival rations gave only seven hundred calories a day and consisted of very small quantities of a variety of concentrated foods. The total ration for one man for ten days weighed about four pounds, and on this meagre diet they dared not take more exercise than was absolutely necessary, although movement would have helped to keep them warm. Their paraffin supply only allowed them a pint and a half of hot fluid each day, so as time went on they became very thirsty indeed.

As the days went by at Shackleton we heard nothing from the Auster's radio, but each morning Taffy sent them a message and listened in case they wished to speak to us. Outside we were working with frantic haste to prepare the Otter for a search. Dividing into day and night shifts so that work could go on throughout the twenty-four hours, the drift which had accumulated inside the wings was melted out with a special hot-air machine, the engine was de-iced and run, and the rudder replaced. By the 29th we were ready and needed only a short period of suitable flying weather, but day after day the wind blew or *whiteout* conditions prevailed—and Gordon and Allan had already spent nine days on the ice shelf.

On the tenth morning they suddenly came through to us on the radio, asking for a weather report from Halley Bay. We had to tell them that visibility was too bad for flying, but added that we were standing by to look for them as soon as conditions improved. They insisted that they were well but admitted feeling 'a bit short of food'. That evening John Lewis was at last able to test-fly the Otter, though low cloud limited its ceiling to five hundred feet and its range to within two or three miles of the base.

On the 30th the weather report from Halley Bay encouraged us to make an attempt; John set off with David Stratton, heading into the dark and murky sky that still brooded over us. But soon they flew into icing conditions which made it impossible for the plane to climb above the cloud, while visibility dropped to a few

---

A *whiteout* is something like a blackout in reverse. A continuous white cloud layer appears to merge with the white snow surface, and it is impossible to tell where one begins and the other ends. No surface irregularities in the snow are visible in the diffused, opaque light, but a dark object like a man or a vehicle may be clearly seen. There is no visible horizon.

hundred yards. Unable to see through the snow squalls they were soon 'ice-berg hopping' at fifty feet, with maximum speed reduced to 75 knots on full throttle, while startled little penguin faces peered anxiously up at the plane which roared so perilously close above. It was obviously much too dangerous to go on and John turned back for base.

That night we were in constant radio touch with Halley Bay, and next morning, hearing that weather conditions had improved, John and David set off once more. Two hours and twenty minutes later they were circling the Royal Society base. Before landing they searched for seventy miles to the south, then went down to refuel before setting off north to the area where we calculated the Auster must have come down.

The aircraft was now radio controlled from Halley Bay, but at Shackleton we could listen-in to the exchanges and soon we heard John reporting that he had picked up the Auster's *SARAH* radio-beacon and, a few minutes later, that he could see a small black speck on the ice. Soon he was safely down and the Auster was being refuelled, while Allan and Gordon had a hot drink ready for them. It was the eleventh day of their ordeal and though they were in good shape, both had lost weight and Gordon was suffering from frostbite. Fifty minutes later the two aircraft were on their way to Halley Bay.

It had taken twelve days to get the doctor there and during that time nature had worked a miraculous cure on Robin Smart, who came down to the airstrip, wondering if *he* would now have a patient on his hands. As Allan climbed out there was some professional uncertainty as to who was supposed to treat who. However, following a mutual examination, each doctor decided that the other was all right, and after resting for two days at Halley Bay our wanderers flew back to Shackleton. At last we were able to turn our eyes to the south, and begin preparations for field work and the relief of South Ice.

The letters *S-A-R-A-H* stand for 'Search Air-Rescue and Homing'.

8. Dogs and dog drivers

Our main journey was planned to start on 14th November, but first we had to find a vehicle route from Shackleton to South Ice, for we knew from flying over the ground that there would be many difficulties with the mountains and the crevasses on the glaciers. We were already seriously behind in our preparations and it was not until 8th October that the Otter was able to relieve the party which had wintered at South Ice. That same evening, David Pratt, Roy Homard, Geoffrey Pratt and I left Shackleton in three Weasels and a Sno-Cat, all towing sledges, feeling our way over the ice shelf.

Next day David Stratton, Ken Blaiklock, Jon Stephenson and George Lowe, with two dog teams, were flown ahead of us to the Shackleton Range. Their task was to find a safe vehicle route up the 'ice wall' which blocked the line of our advance to South Ice, and then to do as much survey and geological work in the mountains as time would permit. Dogs were to be used for this purpose because they are particularly suitable for travelling in mountain areas where tractors cannot travel and aeroplanes cannot land.

The decision to airlift the teams came from the need to save time and to spare the dogs two hundred miles of travelling before reaching the mountain area where they were to start work. A husky's efficiency and endurance is affected over long journeys if he is expected to pull more than 120 lbs., and for this reason the comfortable endurance of a two-team, four-man party is about thirty days.

It took two flights to bring in the dog teams and we were happy to find that they readily took to air travel. Some care was taken to separate known enemies by ration boxes, and one man was perched on top of the sledge, his neck doubled up against the

cabin roof, to prevent fights breaking out between his surrounding passengers. Then the cabin heater was turned full on
to make the animals sleepy—and once John Lewis had accepted
the fact that the lead dog, Nanok, intended to breathe encourag-
ingly down the back of his neck throughout the flight, all was
quiet! Some thirty miles south of Shackleton they flew over our
vehicle party and could see that already one of the Weasels was
jammed in a crevasse. Arriving in the mountains the dogs at
once came to life and after an undignified scuffle over the honour
of disembarking first, they were safely picketed on a rope span.
A depot camp was established from which the two teams worked
during the next three weeks.

From Scott Base dogs were being similarly used, and particularly notable are two journeys, one led by Richard Brooke who,
with Guy Warren, Bernie Gunn and Murray Douglas, travelled
into the mountains north and west of the base, the other being
made by Bob Murray and George Marsh, who pioneered the
route to Depot 700 and then continued on into the unknown
mountains north-west of the Beardmore Glacier.

Brooke's journey followed an intricate route through the mountains for a thousand miles before the party was brought back to
base by air from the Skelton Depot on the Ross Ice Shelf. During
the 126 days they were travelling, twenty-nine mountain-top
survey stations were occupied, besides many others, and they
succeeded in making the first ascent of Mount Huggins, 12,870
feet high. As a result of this journey several large and important
pieces have been fitted into the incomplete jigsaw of Antarctica.

From Depot 700 Bob Miller and George Marsh left the tractor
party to receive the air drop of supplies, and set off with two dog
teams, heading eastward towards the mountains that lie north
and west of the great Beardmore Glacier which had been used
by both Scott and Shackleton as their route to the polar plateau.

It has been said that there is no sport so exhilarating as travelling with a dog team on a fine, clear day. Certainly it is more
exciting and more companionable than roaring steadily along
with unresponsive tractors that show neither enthusiasm nor
boredom, and are restricted to travelling on open snow fields un-
relieved by mountain scenery. There are many ways of making up
a dog team. It may consist of any number of dogs from five to

thirteen, but more normally teams consist of seven or nine. A team of nine, pulling half a ton, is probably the most efficient for long journeys because a larger number consumes so much food that on an extensive trip the extra dogs are only hauling their own rations.

Methods of harnessing dogs and attaching them to the sledge vary with the people of the country and particularly with the nature of the ground over which they are driven. In the Antarctic we used only one type of harness and two types of attachment to the sledge. The harnesses were made of lampwick two inches wide, which is very strong, yet soft, and does not chafe the dogs' bodies.

The two methods of attaching the dogs to the sledge are known as the 'modified fan' and the 'centre trace' systems. The Eskimos use what is called the 'fan', in which every dog has a cord or trace of the same length, attached from the sledge to the harness. This has the advantage that if there are crevasses or cracks in the sea ice and one or more dogs fall through, each can be hauled out on its own trace. The disadvantages are that each dog is breaking a new trail in deep snow and that the direction of pull is not straight forward for all the dogs.

To avoid these troubles the modified fan was developed. In this each pair of dogs has a different length of trace so that only the leader and the front pair break a new trail and the others step in their footprints. In addition they all pull almost straight ahead. Even so, the many long traces are continually getting tangled.

The centre trace is therefore very often more popular with drivers because it is simpler to operate and provides a very straight pull. For bad country the wise driver will also carry a modified fan to which he can change if the dogs are likely to fall into crevasses.

As drivers travel day after day with their dogs, they come to know each individual as a personal friend, and to understand the relationship of each dog to the others in the team. Indeed, so well will they get to know them that if growls or snarls occur at night, a driver can call to the dogs concerned by name without going outside his tent, and probably he will also know which one began the trouble.

Among the dogs themselves each has a definite status which is

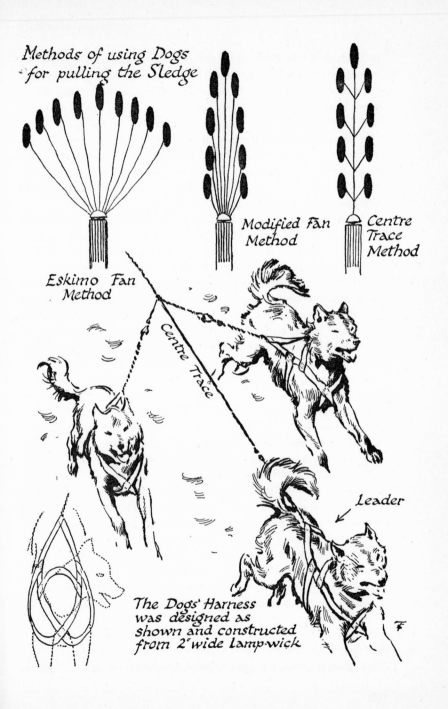

Methods of using Dogs for pulling the Sledge

Eskimo Fan Method

Modified Fan Method

Centre Trace Method

Centre Trace

Leader

The Dogs' Harness was designed as shown and constructed from 2" wide lamp-wick

established by trial of strength. Great friendships spring up between certain dogs, but even then, one is the accepted superior and the other will always lie down if challenged. This 'lying down' is an important matter, for the code of the husky prevents further attack when one dog thus shows that he has given in.

In any team there are two dogs of outstanding importance—the 'leader' and the 'King dog'. The leader is appointed by the driver because he has the intelligence and willingness to obey orders to stop or start, turn left or right, and—quite as important—to keep to a course given by the driver.

The King dog, on the other hand, has himself won his position by strength and cunning. Only rarely will another challenge him, and then only when the challenger thinks he has a chance of ousting him from his position. From a driver's point of view it is useful to have a leader who is also King dog, for when a halt is called and the leader stops, none will dare over-run him. If the King dog is one of the workers behind the leading dog, he, or the rest of the team, will all too often try to reach him to settle an old score. The result is that the leader is unwilling to stop and the driver has difficulty in bringing the sledge to rest.

Sometimes during a long journey a difference arises between two dogs which normally run side by side. Then the driver alters the running order to give the quarrelling pair a change of partners. Known enemies, of course, cannot be run together, and for this reason it is always wise to have one bitch in the team, for she can be used as a partner to any dog which is otherwise difficult to pair off.

A good driver will learn to be a part of the team—to become as it were, 'top dog', and establish that none of the team shall challenge his orders. It is unwise to let either an individual dog or a whole team 'get away' with anything. I have known teams to move off without the driver and return to base on their own. The wise driver will then ski in after them and immediately drive them back over the route they have travelled, to the point where they left him, then turn them round and drive back again.

But if a driver is to be top dog he must himself take the trouble to understand things from a dog's point of view and to follow their line of thought—it is useless for him to expect them to see into his mind. They certainly become expert in interpreting the driver's mood from the tone of his voice, with results that sometimes surprise him. I remember once being annoyed by some event, such as finding it necessary to make a wide detour round an obstacle, and then noticing that on my next command the dogs all looked startled and reacted as though they had done something wrong. This was due to their recognition of displeasure in my voice, about which I was myself entirely unaware.

Another thing a driver must learn is the different appearance of the country from the eye level of the dog. A small island or rocky peak on the horizon may be clearly visible from a man's height but hidden from the dogs. The good driver must remember this, and when directing his leader to a distant point, he must bend right down and make sure that the feature can be seen by his dogs. When the driver has selected the iceberg, mountain or other feature to which he wishes to drive, he conveys the idea to the leading dog by ordering him to left, then right, then left again, until the dog has picked up the object ahead and continues to run towards it.

It is sometimes found that a well-trained leader does not respond to orders given by a new driver. This may partly be due to unwillingness to obey a stranger, but it can also be due to a difference in the pitch of voice. By raising or lowering the pitch to match the voice of the normal driver, the new driver will find that suddenly the team is understanding him. This is one reason why it is unwise to change drivers to suit the convenience of the moment. It is always better to allot a particular team to its own driver.

It is very necessary for a driver to give his orders clearly, loudly, and without confusion of thought or in an excitable manner, for if the dogs do not understand what is wanted and then become frightened by the driver's shouts, chaos will result. At such a time punishment is useless—because the only person who thinks he knows what it is for is the driver!

Naturally, to maintain order among such tough and hardy creatures, punishment is necessary from time to time, but this should be sparingly given and the reason quite clearly understood by the recipient. Again, it is unwise to chastise the leader or King dog if it can be avoided, as there is certainly a 'loss of face' which may provide a great deal more trouble than the punishment has cured. Many people imagine that the long driving whips are used entirely for punishment. In fact they are rarely used for this purpose, particularly when the dogs are being driven in pairs as against the fan method. The whips are carried chiefly to guide the team where sharper turns are required than can be attained by word of command—then the forty-foot long leather thong cast on one side of the team makes the leader turn at a greater angle.

Occasionally a fight develops among all the dogs of a team. This can most easily be dispersed by freely pounding the milling bodies with the thicker part of the whip doubled up as a wide loop, accompanied by much shouting. Sometimes, when one dog team over-runs or veers towards another when passing, an even more difficult situation occurs, for the teams will welcome a fight. Soon eighteen milling bodies, entangled with harnesses and rope traces, make a chaotic and dangerous situation which requires as many hands as are available to break it up. Once a driver has been involved in an inter-team fight, he will make as certain as possible that it will never happen again!

It is from this sort of situation, and from their enjoyment of a fight, that huskies have acquired their reputation for fierceness. In reality, properly treated huskies are very rarely vicious and are insatiable in their desire for affection from anyone who will take notice of them, but a working dog must not be allowed to become too familiar or he will lose all sense of discipline and then be inefficient. Drivers are therefore careful to distribute favours evenly among the team and never allow themselves to make a special favourite.

The dogs themselves develop their own rules, one of which is to avoid fighting while actually hauling a sledge. Woe betide the inexperienced young husky who starts trouble when the team is running, for he will be quickly schooled by those running behind or beside him. If he attempts to turn and face the source of the corrective nip received from behind, he will be turned on his back by the tightening of his trace and then towed ignominiously along upside down.

One of the nicer characteristics of huskies is their great gentleness with puppies. The smaller the puppy the greater the liberties permitted, but this only applies to dogs, for it is only too usual for a bitch to kill puppies belonging to another mother if she can get at them. As the young ones grow older they receive increasing correction from their elders, until they are of full stature and begin to compete with and challenge the older dogs. Then, for the first time, they learn the danger of asserting themselves too much. Even so, when a young dog ten or twelve months old is first run with a team, he is allowed many liberties not permitted to older ones. In many ways his inexperience shows itself. As the team starts its first dash, he will tear along, then unwisely check to look behind him. In a second he finds himself being towed on his back by his trace, and usually the driver must stop the headlong rush so that the learner can regain his feet. Then off again, until once more he somersaults in a swirl of snow.

At last he has the idea, and settles down to pull with the rest of the team. But again, inexperience tells, for the newcomer hauls harder than any, only to become so exhausted after an hour or two that it is as much as he can do to keep running for the last five or six hours of the day. After two or three weeks expending his energy in a wasteful manner, he learns to conserve it, becoming a useful member of the team and no longer leaving the greater part of his work to be done by the older and wiser dogs.

A settled and trained team is usually eager to be off in the morning, but if the country is an uninteresting expanse of flat snow that persists for mile after mile, perhaps day after day, the dogs become bored and it is necessary to keep up their enthusiasm. This can be done by sending one team, then another, into the lead, but this demands equally good leaders in both teams—dogs which will break a new trail, and not all leaders will do this. Another way to hearten a bored team is to change the running pairs, but this can only be done where friendly running companions can be found. Again, a tired team can be greatly encouraged by whistling or singing, but they are quite selective as to the type of song they enjoy. 'Onward Christian Soldiers' is quite effective but 'Show Me the Way to Go Home' is likely to make the dogs break into a run! Whistling has the advantage that it is higher pitched and is therefore preferred by the dogs, but it becomes quite a strain for the driver to continue this for a long time, particularly when travelling into a wind.

A good leader has many qualities besides the will to 'break trail' and the intelligence to obey commands. He will know from experience whether the sea ice is thick enough to bear the team or whether there are crevasses to avoid. If a proper understanding has been established between leader and driver, the dog will convey that the area is dangerous by his reluctance to continue, or by inquiring turns of the head as he slows down. An inexperienced driver may think he knows best and force his team on to thin sea ice, only to see them fall into the water and have to face the reproachful look of his leader, who had all the time been trying to tell him not to make the attempt. There is much that a driver can learn from an experienced leader, and by accepting what is in effect the advice of the dog he will go far towards establishing that essential bond of understanding which makes good driving possible.

Another characteristic of a good leading dog is his sense of direction and his willingness to drive a straight course. Although the driver has the use of a sledge compass, the constant change of orders to run left or right when the leader will not hold a course merely adds to his confusion, and makes steady progress very difficult. In mist or whiteout conditions, when no objects are visible ahead, a good dog is able to maintain a straighter course than is a man ski-ing ahead of the team, because a dog has a much better sense of direction. I remember being a long way from home, and after establishing a depot, turning back to drive an indirect course to base. For five miles I could not convince my leader that he should run the course I wanted—he persisted in running seven degrees to the west of it. When I came to plot our route in the evening, I also plotted the line he had wished to take: it proved to be direct to base a hundred and twenty miles away!

Very often a leader who is breaking trail does not actually do much pulling himself, but leaves this work to the remainder of the team, while he uses his wits to keep the course and find any dangerous places. Behind him, the workers who actually do the hauling do not need to have much sense, and are very often quite stupid. Head down, they strain away, apparently unaware of what goes on ahead of them. Repeatedly they fall through the crevasse lids that the more alert leader and his following pair have carefully jumped! Sometimes a trace will break and a dog is lost in a crevasse, but fortunately this is rare. On one occasion a dog that fell into a crevasse was lucky enough to land on an ice ledge where he stood dazed while we made arrangements to go down

on a rope and recover him. When I reached him, he did not move, but allowed himself to be hoisted unprotesting to the surface. Later, when I went over to speak to him at his place in the team, he came to meet me and licked my hand even though he was not one of my own dogs. I like to think this was his way of saying 'Thank you'—I really believe it was.

Although one may think that the ordinary members of a dog team are not very intelligent, many of them are clever enough to save themselves trouble—in fact to become the real 'old soldier'. A typical example is the dog which learns to keep its trace taut, but yet does no actual pulling. The observant driver can see from the action of the dog's legs that he is not really working. My own cure for this was to attach the slacker close to the front of the sledge, then, when he was not looking, to slip up and sit on the sledge, holding the trace to which he was attached. Gradually I would pull this back, bringing the unsuspecting scrimshanker closer and closer—then a smart smack with the hand on his hindquarters told him that his shirking had been discovered, and he would start to work as he should!

When one stops to camp at the end of the day, the one thought in the mind of every dog is food. As soon as the sledge is securely picqueted, the wise driver will feed his team, for until he does they will snarl and quarrel in anticipation of one perhaps getting something the others have not. If several teams are running together, all must be fed simultaneously or pandemonium will break out, so drivers collect the dog rations together, and then each runs down the line of his own team, giving every dog his allotted pound of pemmican as quickly as possible. Thereafter peace reigns and they settle down to rest.

Yet there is one last routine performance—the Evening Chorus. Nearly always at the end of the day when the drivers are just settling down to sleep, the first short howl provides the prelude to what is coming. In a moment or two every dog has thrown his head high, and in unison, a long-drawn howl fills the air. Then a moment of complete silence while every ear is pricked, listening alertly for an answering call from the wilderness of snow. One repetition of the community cry, and they all curl up to sleep till morning. Sometimes the howl is answered by the teams of another party six or seven miles away—then the exchange persists indefinitely, and the sleepless drivers can only toss restlessly in their sleeping bags.

Such is the background to the journeys of the surveyors and geologists from Shackleton and Scott as they drove their teams up the glaciers and among the mountains on either side of the continent. By the time that Bob Miller and George Marsh had finished their work and returned to Scott Base they had been out in the field for five months and had travelled 1,670 miles—the longest single journey ever made.

I think it is true to say that many tractor drivers have envied the dog men, but I doubt if any dog man would exchange the howls of the teams for the roar of the motors. Many people think that dogs are out of place in modern polar travel, but I do not believe this, for in certain conditions they can do work that neither aircraft nor vehicles can accomplish. Certainly the dogs of the Trans-Antarctic Expedition played their full part in making possible the success of our scientific programme.

9. The route to South Ice

While the dog party completed their survey of a vehicle route up the 'ice wall' and then pushed out into the mountains of the Shackleton Range, we of the four-vehicle reconnaissance party, David Pratt, Roy Homard, Geoffrey Pratt and I, were finding the problems we had to overcome far greater than we had expected. Only eight miles from Shackleton a track roller on Roy's Weasel broke away and jammed between track and sprocket, bending the axle. By eleven o'clock that night we had almost finished removing and replacing the track, but it could only be a temporary repair, and by noon the next day a very disappointed Roy was on his way back to base. Like the ten little nigger boys—now there were three!

On the third day I found myself driving up a rough snow slope, then suddenly near the crest it was apparent that I was moving over a succession of covered crevasses. None of us then had any idea how thick a 'snow bridge' should be to bear the weight of a Weasel, a Sno-Cat, or even a sledge. We were making a good speed of 8 m.p.h., the Weasels bucking over the rough surface, when narrow holes appeared every few yards where the tracks broke through the small crevasse bridges. Periodically we examined these and always found them narrow and harmless, but our rising feeling of confidence was soon curbed when a small dark hole suddenly appeared about thirty yards ahead. As I gazed at it my Weasel gave an uncomfortable sinking lurch and stopped abruptly—with the $2\frac{1}{2}$-ton sledge tilted sideways through the broken snow bridge of a crevasse.

Until a few moments before the others had been following close behind, and I climbed out thinking they would be there to help, but they were in worse trouble a quarter of a mile back. Returning to them on skis, I found that a snow bridge which I had safely crossed had collapsed under David Pratt's Weasel. To recover it we passed a rope from the Sno-Cat over the top of the Weasel and shackled it to rings on the far side. We were then able to haul it into an upright position, although the fallen track still hung over the abyss. Finally, using my vehicle (which we had first recovered from its lesser predicament), the front of the Weasel was towed slightly to one side until David could drive clear on the one track still resting on firm snow. By one o'clock in the morning we had also managed to extract my sunken sledge and had radioed John Lewis at Shackleton asking for the Auster to come out later in the day, and also for Roy Homard to join us and strengthen our party. Clearly we were soon likely to encounter serious trouble if we did not use air reconnaissance to help us past the difficult places.

At our camp we could hear constant noise due to movement of the ice below. In one crevasse the staccato metallic sound of breaking ice made us imagine two men building a metal shed in the dark depths beneath, while another, about five feet from my tent, was even louder, sounding as though a team of boilermakers was at work.

Next morning John and Roy arrived, the Auster 'homing' on to our SARAH beacon and coming down on a flagged strip a hundred yards long. We had difficulty in finding a safe stretch, and even in that short distance the landing was made at right angles across eight crevasses. Flying over the area with John I could see that we were heading into a really bad patch and that our only course was to withdraw and strike west through the narrowest part of the crevassed area, before turning south once more.

We now had to strike camp, turn the sledges round, rope the vehicles together (using Terylene safety lines with a breaking strain of fifteen tons) and go back the way we had come. The surrounding crevasses made this a long and laborious task for we had to find safe areas where there was sufficient room for the vehicles to turn without falling into the holes which lay in wait all round them.

At last all was safely accomplished, and we began our first attempt at driving the vehicles roped together like climbers on a mountain. From the rear of each Weasel a double steel wire rope passed under the sledge behind, to be attached to sixty-five feet of 3-inch Terylene rope linked with the front of the next vehicle. This served as a safety rope to hold any tractor that fell into a crevasse and also allowed the leading vehicle to aid the one behind it if more power was needed to pull it out of a difficult place.

Driving roped together is not easy, for the rope must not be so taut as to restrict the rapid acceleration of the vehicle in front, nor must it be so loose on the surface that it is run over and snapped by the tracks of the following vehicle; indeed it is possible for a rope to break a track. Later we were to acquire very considerable skill in 'roped driving', but on this occasion our maximum speed was $3\frac{1}{2}$ m.p.h.

Next day we set off on a new course, and in spite of high drift and a stop to repair a fractured oil pipe on David's Weasel, we had travelled twenty-five miles by the evening. The following day there was no visibility but we ploughed on by compass. After ten miles a slight 'tick' in my Weasel engine was noticeably increasing and we discovered this to be a 'run' big-end. This was disastrous, for we could not now turn back, and even in a workshop the repair would take three days. After discussion we decided to short-circuit the plug and drive on for as long as the engine lasted. My load was lightened by filling all tanks and half-empty barrels on the other sledges, and we abandoned three fuel drums to act as a depot for our next run. We had now reached 79°00′S, 37°40′W.

Setting off again, with the damaged Weasel limping ahead, we travelled another thirty miles, over a surface that had become gradually rougher and more undulating. On the third evening the pall of cloud broke and allowed the sun to light up the mountains of the Shackleton Range fifty miles away.

All day the Weasels had been labouring through a recent fall of soft snow that hid hard sastrugi running across our course. These made the vehicles and sledges heave and plunge like small ships at sea, their tracks churning out a white spray of snow. The Sno-Cat sailed majestically like a battleship over the wavy surface, its four independent tracks fitting themselves easily to the rough ridges.

112

Sno-Cat 'Able' before Mount Huggins

Mount Harmsworth, 9,500 ft, from the Skelton Glacier.
Climbed by the Geological Party from Scott Base

Sno-Cat 'Haywire' on the Skelton Glacier, Mount Huggins in the background

Looking across the open water of McMurdo Sound
to the Western Mountains

Camp on 'The Portal', entrance to the Skelton Glacier, late February 1958

Emperor penguins watch the loading of H.M.N.Z.S. *Endeavour* at Scott Base

Sunset over the
Western Mountains

As two 'U' bolts on David's Weasel had broken, we spent the next day in repair and maintenance. While the engineers worked on the vehicles, Geoffrey and I laid out the seismic equipment and fired four separate shots to find out the thickness of the ice shelf. During the morning we spoke by radio to David Stratton and Ken Blaiklock, who had by now completed the route reconnaissance of the high ice wall ahead, and they gave us precise instructions about the course they had flagged up it. But we knew that before we reached the wall we should enter a complex area of crevasses which could not be avoided.

Suddenly, on 19th October, after travelling thirty-five miles, our vehicles began to break numerous small holes in the surface. David Pratt again found the largest, and with a roar from his Weasel's engine bounced across to stop with the vehicle on one side and the sledge on the other. Recovery was a simple matter of disconnecting the sledge, towing it away from the crevasse and hitching up again. We now roped up the vehicles and continued cautiously at 3 m.p.h. Whenever I felt a snow bridge sag beneath my Weasel, I waved to David behind, and he in turn waved to Geoffrey, each of them moving slightly to one side to cross at a fresh point. I had decided to halt at 8.15 p.m. but, with only one minute to go, there was a sudden backward lurch as my Weasel tilted steeply upwards and jerked to a stop; peering out I found myself suspended over a dark abyss that widened downwards in all directions. The back of the Weasel was resting against the edge of the crevasse on its rear floatation tank, and was held in that position by the sledge towbar; only the first bogey and the very front of the tracks were lodged on the far side, but I climbed out safely after the others had cheerfully photographed my predicament.

The four of us probed the whole area to find the shape and extent of the cavern I had revealed. Although the surface all round the big crevasse was riddled with smaller ones, we decided that it was possible to cross it fifteen yards to the left. Geoffrey then drove his Sno-Cat over, together with two sledges, unhitched and came back for my Weasel. Using a wire rope he hauled the Weasel forward while I lay over the back and lifted the sledge towbar clear of the towing hook. This left the front of the sledge overhanging the brink of the crevasse, so I drove back over the safe route, pulled it clear, manœuvred to hitch on again and rejoined Geoffrey and Roy on the far side. By the time David joined us with his Weasel it was ten o'clock and we decided we had had enough for one day. Quickly we probed the snow surface to find secure places for our tents, and settled down for the night.

Very often the recovery of a vehicle was not the time-consuming factor; it was the examination of the surrounding area to give us room to manœuvre which took so long. This was particularly the case when all the vehicles and sledges had to be turned round in places where the crevasses were so close that tracks had to run along the length of a crevasse instead of at right angles to it. The time taken to turn three vehicles and their sledges round would be perhaps three or four hours, while the actual recovery of the one in trouble would be under half an hour.

Since the previous day we had had difficult radio conditions and could not tell Shackleton of our urgent need for more air reconnaissance, so I spent 21st October probing the snow every yard of the way for one and a half miles ahead, marking a possible track around the worst places for a move next day if the plane did not arrive. The 22nd was beautifully sunny with a clear sky, visibility of forty miles and the temperature $-26°F$. Unhappily, radio communication was at its worst and we again made no contact with base. I therefore decided to continue, but with little success. In spite of careful probing my Weasel broke through within twenty yards of starting, but hauled itself out on the far side. Then, as David pulled to one side to avoid the hole, I went deep into another. More probing was now necessary before the Sno-Cat could draw ahead to tow me out. Everywhere there were endless cracks, all hidden by surface sastrugi, and though the plunging of our poles gave a drum-like sound where there were crevasses, the same noise was made in many places by solid *windcrust* layers buried beneath the surface. It seemed a hopeless task to force a route for many miles over such country; great was our relief, therefore, when we made contact with Shackleton

---

Windcrust is a hard snow layer formed on the surface by the wind compacting together the crystals. Usually not more than six inches thick. A man walking on hard windcrust will leave no footprints.

early in the afternoon and heard that the weather was good enough for the Auster to fly out to us immediately. When my Weasel had been recovered, the vehicles and sledges were left where they were until I could decide from the forthcoming flight whether or not we had to turn back.

That afternoon John Lewis arrived in the Auster, rather cold after his two-hundred-mile flight from Shackleton in the un-heated cockpit. After stamping around for a few moments to restore circulation, he announced that he was ready to go. Circling over the vehicles it was immediately clear that a really badly broken area lay ahead of us and that once again we must make another attempt elsewhere. Flying east we could see that the narrowest part of this crevassed belt was ten to eleven miles wide, and that evening I wrote in my journal:

> If we can break through that belt we have a chance of good going beyond. It will certainly be a tough job and a dangerous one, but if we are to have a trans-Antarctic journey it has to be attempted, and somehow we must be successful.

Flying back to the vehicles, I told John that we should need to set up a close support Air Camp and that a suitable point seemed to be a site at the foot of the Shackleton Range. This would be only about twenty miles away from us, and also near enough for the plane to assist the dog parties if necessary. With the aircraft so close, it would be working with us in our weather conditions, instead of relying on the more variable coastal weather at Shackleton.

We refuelled the plane and John left for base, his feet colder than ever, while we set about hauling our vehicles and sledges from their holes. This was finished by nine o'clock, when the temperature had fallen to −40°F and we were all glad to pitch our tents in almost the same place as the previous night. That morning we had moved fifty yards forward—in the evening we went a hundred yards back!

Next morning we started our return trek with all the vehicles roped together. I am not sure whether it is more unpleasant to rumble back over the gaping holes one has previously left behind, or to break new ground, wondering when the next sickening lurch will herald the discovery of a new crevasse. It was David Pratt who said pessimistically that driving the vehicles over the booming caverns reminded him of driving a tank over a mine-field, except that in this case he was waiting for something to go down and not up!

Apart from a few small breakthroughs, we made fairly easy progress on a new course which took us to the narrowest part of the crevassed area where, I had decided from the air, we must attempt our crossing. The Air Camp was to be established that evening and in my journal I find:

> In my opinion the next ten miles are going to make or break the expedition, for we may well lose vehicles over the ground close ahead. With crash helmets, safety straps and roped vehicles we have taken all the precautions we can.

In our tent that night David and I listened in to a four-way radio conversation between the two aircraft flying in to establish the Air Camp, Shackleton, and Geoffrey Pratt, who was operating our transmitter from his Sno-Cat. Talking to base Geoffrey identified himself as, 'Hallo Shackleton—this is "Haywire" calling'. From that moment his Sno-Cat, containing all the seismic equipment, was always known as 'Haywire'.

In the morning Gordon Haslop and George Lowe arrived in the Auster. I went up for a low-level reconnaissance of the sur-rounding area and then flew on to look at the route up the ice wall flagged for us by the survey dog party. I was appalled to see that while the track led straight up a slope of the ice wall, it crossed a maze of very large filled crevasses. After a close ex-amination of the only alternative route nearer the mountains, I decided that that was even more difficult and that we must follow our fortunes along the line of little red and black flags that fluttered below.

The next ten miles would be difficult for our vehicles, and we decided to probe the surface every yard for the whole distance to ensure that we found and investigated each hidden crack. I wrote in my journal:

> It has been a very slow task, but some of the monstrous caverns which we have discovered beneath the innocent

117

surface have certainly justified the work. Some of them would have accepted a double-decker bus, and there is no doubt that we should have lost at least one Weasel if we had not spent so much time on the ground. . . .

At first the weather was excellent, and each day the Auster flew one or other of us low over the area immediately ahead, while the ground party continued the endless, step-by-step probing and flagging of the route. On the 27th however there was a whiteout and no flying was possible. We therefore lined up stakes with a compass and worked towards each other in pairs, each of us separated from his partner by a distance slightly greater than the width of the vehicle tracks. Shuffling forward, each man plunged his wooden or aluminium pole to a depth of five feet every yard—a distance sometimes reduced to a foot or six inches if there was reason to suspect the area. When a crevasse was found the cracks along its edges were opened up at several points, so that we could examine the filling. If it appeared unsafe to cross, a diversion would be made to avoid the dangerous part. These diversions were marked by arrows drawn in the snow some way before the turn-off was reached; sometimes stakes, flags or ski sticks were used to draw attention to such points. Rules of the road were developed, and drivers had always to leave the arrows or flags on their left—all vehicles were left-hand drive— and travel with their tracks within one foot of the markers.

The latest date for our arrival at South Ice was to have been 28th October—yet, on that day, we were still among crevasses on the ice shelf, at least a hundred and fifty miles away. That day we had covered two and a quarter miles and felt that we were almost clear of the worst crevasses. There was an enormous temptation to get into the vehicles and drive on hoping for the best, but after all the care we had taken in getting ourselves over an area which we believed to be the worst ever attempted by vehicles, it would have been a pity to make a mistake in the last stages—so we probed carefully on.

That night we heard from base that there had been an accident to the Auster. Gordon had been flying in support of the survey party and on 28th October David Stratton had asked to be taken up a glacier with a message for Jon Stephenson and Taffy

Williams who, with a dog team, were 'geologizing' in the mountains. As the plane appeared over them Jon and Taffy both gazed upwards to watch it land. Unfortunately their leader and team did the same, with the result that they all, men, dogs and sledge, plunged over a steep snow bank about two hundred feet high. A confusion of barking dogs and shouting men rolled down the slope to within a few yards of the bottom. At the same moment the Auster landed close by and David Stratton, almost helpless with laughter, was in time to run across and help right the sledge. Taffy and Jon were indignant but unhurt, and the huskies, who had taken the opportunity to start a free-for-all, seemed quite pleased with the incident.

However, the dog party were to have the last laugh. Five minutes later, Gordon and David taxied away to begin the take-off towards the nunataks. With an upward slope and two men in the little plane, all was not well, and the account in David's journal reads:

> . . . it was soon obvious that we were not going to be able to gain sufficient height to clear the snow and ice ridge by the side of the nunatak, and sure enough we gave the crest a number of good heavy glancing blows, then fluttered down into the hollow which presented itself on the other side. Unfortunately this was neither deep nor long enough to allow us to gain flying speed and full control, and it became apparent that we were bumping and boring into the windscoop by the side of the nunatak, with a 200-ft. ice wall at the head of it. At this point Gordon took the only possible course—cut his engine, and we bumped and slithered along on the side of the windscoop, running parallel to the rock wall. It seemed to take an interminable time to reduce speed, and as we did so a boulder appeared right ahead. Hard-a-port meant descent on to the rocky scree ten yards to our left, and hard-a-starboard meant ascending the side of the windscoop. Gordon chose the latter, and as we made a violent lurch up the hill, the tail ski jammed in a small meltwater crack and was torn off, bringing us to an abrupt halt. . . .

Fortunately the occupants were safe enough, but over the ridge behind, Jon and Taffy were having a very anxious time, for they had seen the plane hit the ridge and then disappear, without any further sight or sound. Racing to the top of the slope, they were relieved to see it perched safely, but precariously, like a fly on the steep wall of the windscoop. Peter Weston was at once flown in by the Otter to do repairs, and we realized that for a time the vehicle reconnaissance party would have no further air support. Happily this was to prove unnecessary, for the very next day we cleared the last of the crevasses and motored steadily for twelve miles over a smooth surface towards the snow cairn that marked the start of the ascent up the ice wall.

Here we roped up the vehicles and began to follow the flags at the foot of the steep main slope. At first all went well, then my Weasel sank into the soft snow until the underneath of the body was resting on the surface and the tracks could get no grip. After much digging and a number of useless attempts to get clear, Geoffrey had to bring forward Haywire to pull me out. Immediately afterwards the same thing happened to David's Weasel. The slope was proving hard on my damaged engine, which had been making more and more ominous noises, so, hitching my sledge as a third behind the Sno-Cat, I now moved on alone and unroped. Slowly and cautiously I crept higher and higher until I crossed a wide crevasse which marked the top of the ice wall. From here and in the far distance below me, I could see a thin trail extending away across the snow to the east, and could make out a tiny black dot at the head of it—a dog team was coming over to us from the Air Camp nineteen miles away. Soon they had caught us up and that night David Stratton and Ken Blaiklock camped with us.

By now I was becoming seriously concerned about the amount of work which remained to be done at base, where Ralph Lenton and the others were preparing stores and material for the main journey. A great deal of work remained to be done on the rest of the vehicles, and it was essential that one of the engineers should return to Shackleton for that purpose. The next day, therefore, Roy Homard and Ken left with the dog team, to return to the Air Camp whence Roy could fly back to base. David Stratton remained with the vehicles to guide us over the rest of the selected route.

Two events made 30th October a bad day. After half a mile

my poor Weasel finally stopped with a broken camshaft drive and had to be abandoned. This involved reloading and relashing our sledges, for the less essential items had to be left behind. Now— two little nigger boys—we found that the way led past some very large, heavily bridged crevasses. One of these, about forty feet wide, was marked with a red and white chequered flag, showing that it had appeared dangerous to the dog party when they had passed that way. But after examining it we decided we must cross somehow. David's Weasel, now in the lead, sank in the soft snow, so Geoffrey drove Haywire across, unhitched his sledges, and returned to pull the Weasel and its load.

While this was being done David S. was standing on the far side, I on the near side of the crevasse, while Geoffrey and David P. were driving. As they moved across I heard a tremendous rumble and the snow beneath me quaked, making me want to move rapidly to some other place, but as I had no idea where the noise originated, I stood where I was. As the vehicles continued to move slowly, I saw a cloud of snow rising in the air from an immense crater which had appeared only six feet to the left of the Weasel. It was about 20 feet across and 40 feet deep, with dark and deep caverns descending to unknown depths. For a long time clouds of snow dust rose from it and drifted away, the whole thing appearing as though a bomb had fallen. The hole was large enough to have swallowed Sno-Cat, Weasel, sledges and all, but with amazing good fortune the bridge broke to the left of the vehicles and not under them! After taking photographs we proceeded chastened on our way. . . .

That evening the Otter flew over our camp on its way to South Ice and dropped us four cooked steaks, which made a welcome change from the interminable pemmican which, although highly nutritious, no one likes very much. John Lewis made an excellent bombing run, the package with its red streamers to help us pick it out in the snow landing only ten yards from Haywire. In the morning we cleared the last of the crevassed zone at the top of the ice wall, and came to the end of the trail flagged for us. We were now only four miles from the foot of the Shackleton Range and

continued unroped for a few miles, when suddenly we found that we were crossing the snow bridges of a number of very wide crevasses. Cautiously we moved closer to the mountains.

Soon we were travelling within half a mile of the rocky spurs, while all the time the surface rose steeply to the south, and the vehicles ground along in low gear. The climb became ever steeper and we met huge sastrugi that rose four and five feet above the level of the surface. By the evening we had rounded the corner of the range and were ploughing along at an altitude of nearly three thousand feet.

Next day was a maintenance day, which we spent in tightening the Weasel's tracks, in greasing and in changing all oils—a very cold task with the temperature down to −35°F and the wind blowing at ten knots. By five o'clock in the evening we were ready to start on the crossing of the Recovery Glacier, and we headed towards the Whichaway Nunataks, hoping every moment that they would appear over the horizon. On and on we went,

topping one rise after another, but always it was a false horizon. From air reconnaissance we knew that somewhere ahead there was a great belt of crevasses, but I had observed one or two places where these appeared to be covered with snow, and it was towards one of these gaps that we were now feeling our way.

By 2nd November we were stopped by a maze of hummocks through which it was clearly going to be very difficult to make any headway at all. Ski-ing ahead to search for a route, we found ourselves surrounded by a forest of these hummocks up to fifteen feet high, while between them a mosaic of crevasses seemed to run in every direction. The whole area had a queer 'lost world' effect, as though one was wandering in some region of the moon.

Knowing that the Otter was likely to be flying to South Ice, I called Shackleton and asked John Lewis to divert a few miles and make a reconnaissance of the area so that he could suggest which way we should turn to find a gap in this new obstacle. We then pitched our tents and waited for the plane. It duly arrived in the evening and John and Ken Blaiklock, who was with him, advised us to move five miles to the east where there seemed to be a possible route. Quickly striking camp, we moved to the area indicated and began a careful examination on skis, only to find that there, too, the ground was heavily crevassed. The plane had now flown on to South Ice and, having discharged its load, would later be returning to base. We therefore pitched our tents once more and asked for another air reconnaissance on the return flight. At one o'clock in the morning David Stratton and I were still refuelling the vehicles when the Otter again circled the area and Ken Blaiklock said he could see a much better point five miles further to the east. Shortly afterwards John landed and Ken handed over the sketch he had made of the crevassed area ahead of us. As the temperature was then —40°F they were as glad to climb back into the warm aircraft as we were to scramble into our tents.

Next morning we travelled to the suggested area and ski-ed forward to examine the ground. I was dismayed to find the well-known 'basin' or tadpole-shaped depressions which we knew so well as representing short, wide crevasses completely covered with snow lids. So it proved, and we took five days to force a passage across this narrow belt of eleven miles.

Now that we had only two vehicles left, we had to take even greater care, for the loss of one would place us in a very dangerous position, and although the Sno-Cat could recover the Weasel, there was very little hope of the Weasel helping the 'cat' out of a hole.

On the second day we moved forward only half a mile after probing every yard of the route, but even so the Weasel broke through twice in a hundred yards, and the second time we very nearly lost it altogether, for it hung precariously lengthwise along a crevasse bridge which had already broken along one side. It was only possible to pull it out along the length of the bridge, and so certain were we that it was going down that every useful item was carefully unloaded before the attempt was made. When at last we were successful, it was a great sight to see David's beaming face, for it was his Weasel and he had been quite certain that it would not be recovered.

At this time our rate of progress was so slow that the date of our arrival at South Ice was becoming more and more uncertain. Owing to the treacherous surface it was impossible for the plane to land anywhere in our area, but I asked for more food to be dropped to us on the next flight. On the evening of 5th November the Otter circled our camp three times, on each occasion dropping two bundles of rations, which gave us an ample reserve. The temperature at our altitude was now always low, and when we finished work each night it was $-35°F$ to $-40°F$. When there was a brisk breeze as well, conditions were very uncomfortable as we prodded our way slowly onwards. When we came to undress in the evenings, stockings, outer duffels, three pairs of foot duffels and the thick felt and plastic insoles would be frozen to the inside of the moccasins in one solid mass of rime and ice.

Each long and tiring day of prodding took us forward only half a mile. We developed two different techniques—either we used thin aluminium tubes six feet long to probe through the layers of snow and ice, and assumed the area safe if there was still resistance at the full depth of the thrust; or we used the ice chisels mounted on solid wooden poles—by plunging with the butt end, a crevasse bridge would reverberate loudly, and these we came to call 'boomers'. Then, using the chisel end, a hole would be cut and enlarged until it was possible to thrust one's head, and sometimes shoulders, far enough through the lid to see the width and direction of the cavern underneath. Hanging head down over a bottomless pit with sloping blue-white sides disappearing into the depths, gave the impression of gazing into clear, deep water—but this can be somewhat alarming when you know that very soon you will be driving a 2- or 3-ton vehicle, together with heavy sledges, over the precarious snow bridges above the abyss. We certainly learnt to take a great interest in each other's probing!

By the end of the 6th, we had prepared another half-mile of the route and were bringing forward the vehicles over what seemed safe ground, when there was a rumbling noise like underground thunder and at the same time a shuddering and gentle collapse of the whole snow surface. Then, before our eyes, two enormous holes, thirty to forty feet long and twelve feet wide, appeared on either side of the track just ahead of the vehicles. They stopped quickly!

Vibration had caused the bridge of a crevasse just ahead of the vehicles to fall in, but along the probed route it had stood firm. After further examination David Pratt cautiously led on with his Weasel, but fifty yards further on he suddenly plunged through a snow bridge six feet thick, and remained precariously suspended by the very front of the vehicle and by a short length of track at the rear. Had the crevasse been six inches wider he would certainly have fallen headlong down, to hang suspended by the safety rope attached to the Sno-Cat behind. By midnight, when the 'cat' had pulled him out backwards, there was a semi-white-out and we were very tired, so we camped where we were, surrounded by the gaping holes for which our passage had been responsible.

The Recovery Glacier had many more unpleasant surprises for us; first a series of wide but filled chasms as much as a hundred feet across. These we examined carefully and suspiciously, but in fact they gave us no trouble at all and it was not long before we were attempting the crossing of a curious belt of snow hills as much as eighty feet high. These formed a continuous line along the length of the glacier for many many miles. Between each pair of hills was an enormous deep pit, many of them twenty to thirty yards across, and apparently bottomless. These pits were the exposed parts of very large crevasses which were otherwise filled with snow or bridged by the great windblown drifts which formed the hills we had to cross.

When we came to prospect a route over one of these hills we found that the surface was firm and hardly at all crevassed, and the vehicles passed over quite uneventfully. The next major difficulty was a very badly crevassed area about two miles wide, on the very edge of the Recovery Glacier where it passed along the foot of the Whichaway Nunataks. After many miles of reconnaissance on ski and on foot, we were compelled to move five miles to the west before we could find a safe way through, and even this route was to give us a great deal of trouble when we came to cross it for the second time in December. Now, however, we gained the far side without undue difficulty, and began to climb the relatively smooth glacier coming down between the most easterly of the rocky nunataks.

Our camp that night was at 4,000 feet, almost a thousand feet above the Recovery Glacier, and less than a mile from the nearest rocks. Unfortunately we had no time to visit them but all the work that we had to do there had been completed by Jon Stephenson when he and Ken Blaiklock had been landed at the nunataks by air in March. South Ice was now only about thirty miles away and we determined that we must get there the next day, 13th November.

The going was rough across the wide area of high sastrugi ridges, but at least we had little to fear from crevasses now that we were on the more open snow fields beyond the nunataks. As we moved towards the station we kept in constant touch with Hal Lister and Hannes La Grange who were living there. When we were still some miles distant, Hal set out on skis to meet us, and presently we saw a dark dot on the horizon which came and went as we dipped into the hollows or rose to the top of ridges. Then suddenly, there he was close over the top of a ridge, but what should have been the splendid moment of our meeting was somewhat spoiled in the last few yards, for David's Weasel ran out of petrol and Hal collapsed in a flailing heap as his skis caught under the sastrugi!

When at last we reached South Ice, another three and a half miles on, we were welcomed by Hannes, who came hastening out to meet us, and the excited yelping of the dogs tethered not far from the buried station. It had taken us thirty-seven days and four hundred miles to reach South Ice; we flew back to Shackleton in two and a half hours. Nine days later we started all over again!

10. The depot-laying journey from Scott Base

The Ross Sea Party at Scott Base were more fortunate than we at Shackleton for the better spring weather enabled them to begin field work early in September. By the middle of October their dog teams had all been brought to the peak of condition during short trips around the base, and it was time for the main southern journey to lay the depots for the Crossing Party. The original plan had been to use dog teams for this, but Ed Hillary decided that his little Ferguson tractors should make at least the first stages of the journey. He had the full support of Murray Ellis and Jim Bates, the engineers who had worked so hard during the winter to prepare them for this attempt, but otherwise few people in McMurdo Sound believed they would ever get very far from base!

On 14th October, Ed, Murray Ellis, Ron Balham and Peter Mulgrew drew up the little convoy—three Fergusons and a Weasel—hitched on the sledges, waved goodbye to their companions, and drove slowly away from Scott Base. They hauled a total load of over ten and a half tons, although they realized that the Fergusons were not powerful enough to cope with this over soft surfaces or in deep snow. Barely five miles from base the first tractor pulled up with a jerk and Ed found that one of his sledges had broken through a crevasse bridge and was tilted over at an alarming angle. This meant unloading the twelve large fuel drums lashed on to it, while a tractor took the strain and prevented the sledge falling further. By the time it was safely out and reloaded, the day was over and they pitched their first camp only six and a half miles from base.

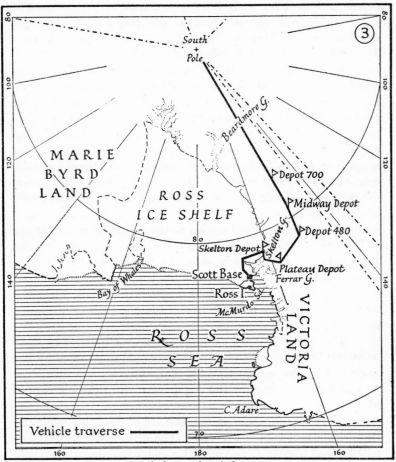

Vehicle traverse ———

Royal Geographical Society

The second day was fine and mild with the temperature at
— 12°F, but soon they found themselves in deep soft snow. One
tractor after another bogged down completely and in the first
two hours they covered only one mile. Already it was time for
drastic action. They unloaded eight drums of fuel to be left
behind, thus reducing the load by one and a half tons. This
enabled them to keep moving and at the end of a long day's
driving they had covered twenty-three miles.

In the next few days the temperature again dropped to the
minus thirties, the surface improved, and they were able to do
more than thirty miles each day. The Weasel, although much
better able to plough its way through soft snow than the Fergusons, was giving a great deal of mechanical trouble and was
already in need of major repairs. As they reached an area of high
sastrugi off Minna Bluff, the snow surface became hard and firm
which made all the difference to the little Fergusons, but now the
Weasel was labouring with its heavier load, and had to work very
hard to keep up.

On 19th October John Claydon in the Beaver flew Bob Miller
and George Marsh, with two dog teams, from Scott Base to the
Skelton Depot, thus cutting off nearly two hundred miles from
their journey south. The next day the tractor party also arrived
at this depot amid howls of welcome from the teams. They had
covered the last fifty miles in thirteen hours, their ears attuned
to the monotonous drone of the engines and the cold creeping
through their thick down clothing as they sat huddled in their
unheated cabs. Every three hours they would stop to make a hot
drink in the comparative warmth of the caboose, and they were
very glad to be greeted by the dog drivers with steaming cups of
tea.

For two days the whole party remained at the depot while the
engineers worked on the Weasel. The drive shaft for the dis-
tributor had fractured, making it necessary to remove the whole
engine to make the repair. To do so, baulks of timber brought
for possible crevasse rescue operations were used to build a rough
bipod over the vehicle. From this they slung a pulley and chain
so that the motor could be lifted out of its bed and the broken part
mended.

On the morning of the 22nd the dog drivers loaded their

sledges, hitched up their teams, and started on the long climb up the glacier. By late afternoon the vehicle repairs had been completed and at five o'clock the tractor party followed. The icy slopes were extremely rough and the dog men had a hard day, for the sledges constantly overturned on the slippery surface. That night two very tired drivers climbed into their sleeping bags.

The Fergusons following behind did well, but the sledges were wracked and twisted. Then, late that night, the weather closed down and a violent wind obscured the scene with drifting snow. The next day mist, snow and occasional sudden squalls of up to fifty knots, made travelling impossible. There was a complete whiteout, and walking around the camp was a hazardous business that caused many a tumble over invisible sastrugi. By noon on the following day the weather had improved a little and they decided to make an attempt to travel. The dogs were the first off, and soon disappeared into a cloud of driving drift. Half an hour later the tractors moved off and had barely travelled a hundred yards before they in turn were enveloped in swirling, blinding snow. They could hardly see where they were going, but by the end of the first hour they had covered five miles and came out on to the clear ice of the middle portion of the Skelton Glacier where they received the full force of the wind. It was impossible to stand on the slippery surface without keeping a firm grip on a tractor or sledge, but at least the wind had swept away all the snow, and it was now possible to see!

Anxiously they looked for the dog teams, but they were nowhere to be seen. Ed drove back some way trying to find them, and then came to the conclusion they must have stopped and camped farther back. The vehicles battled on into the gale for another two hours, then, as they reached an area of narrow crevasses, the wind fortunately moderated. Although the crevasses were not large enough to engulf a tractor, it was tedious work finding a winding route over the narrowest points, and often the bridges broke as the vehicles lurched across, leaving gaping holes behind them. That night they were glad to camp on firm snow.

Ahead, the Skelton Glacier rose in two great sweeps which they called the Lower and Upper Staircase, with a flat area in the

131

middle known as the Landing. Next morning they began the laborious climb. Dodging crevassed areas they made height steadily and only on the steepest slopes was it necessary to relay their loads. In bright sunlight and a light wind, by the end of the day they had crossed the Lower Staircase and pitched their camp on the Landing at a height of 2,680 feet, having covered twelve miles. They were concerned for the dog drivers as most of the rations for them were being carried in the vehicles, so Ed decided to wait on the Landing until the teams had caught up. It was a good opportunity to carry out vehicle maintenance.

During the afternoon they were relieved to hear the cries of the dog drivers as the teams came toiling into camp. Soon after the parties had separated, Bob and George had been forced to camp in the storm: later, they found from the tracks in the snow that the tractors had passed within thirty feet without seeing them, because of the all-enveloping drift.

Next morning there were more difficulties. A rapid rise in temperature to 0°F was accompanied by a day of snowfall and mist. They had set the alarum for an early start, but at 4.45 a.m. it was still very thick outside. In spite of this they prepared to leave, but conditions were almost impossible, with complete cloud cover causing a whiteout. The area immediately ahead was known to be crevassed so the dog teams went first to reconnoitre a safe route. The tractors followed an hour later, but it was a day of fumbling over invisible surfaces, of rock bluffs appearing and disappearing, and of constant tension and worry. They followed the dog tracks for many miles, although it was often necessary to get out of the tractors and peer closely at the snow to pick them out. At one point they lost the tracks altogether, and had to feel their own way carefully among the crevasses, relaying their loads over the steeper stretches from the Upper Staircase to the slope running on to the Skelton Névé. That night both parties camped at 5,000 feet and the worst was over.

During the night the wind freshened and next morning it was bitterly cold. Conditions were impossible for dog teams, but believing they were now clear of crevasses, Ed took the tractors forward, driving into the teeth of the wind, with heavy drift blotting out the landscape and the temperature in the minus thirties. In three hours they had climbed the last of the steep slopes and were travelling on the comparatively easy gradient of the névé.

After the lunch halt there was a roar overhead and John Claydon was seen circling above them in the Beaver. He had just landed Harry Ayres and Roy Carlyon with a dog team at Plateau Depot, where they were now pitching their camp. The remainder of their gear, and another team, would be flown in as soon as weather permitted. It was good to know that everything was going so well, and as John flew away to Scott Base, the tractor party drove on towards the rim of the névé.

For two more days they suffered strong winds, heavy drifts and cold temperatures as they hauled their loads up over the hard, rough slope leading from the Skelton Névé to the high plateau. On 30th October, in a temperature of $-33°F$ and winds gusting to fifty knots, they only managed two and a half miles, fighting every inch of the way. But next day things were better. The thermometer rose to $-20°F$ and as it was fine and sunny Ed could fix his position accurately from the surrounding peaks and the sun. Then the mist came down again and it was difficult to steer an accurate course through the rough sastrugi, but they knew they must be fast approaching Plateau Depot. That evening a small black triangle appeared several miles ahead of them which could only be the tent of Harry and Roy, and before long the vehicles once more drove into camp. They were now two hundred and ninety miles from Scott Base and on the plateau at last, at an altitude of 8,200 feet. In getting so far they felt that the Fergusons had already more than repaid the labours of the winter.

Soon afterwards, Bob Miller and George Marsh, with their two teams, joined the camp. Although the tractors had travelled almost three hundred miles to get there, Plateau Depot was only ten miles nearer to the South Pole than Scott Base, as can be seen from the map on page 129. However, they had arrived with eighteen drums of petrol and sufficient food and paraffin to cover the whole summer's operations and Ed now had no hesitation about taking the vehicles farther south. John Claydon and Bill Cranfield started flying in load after load of supplies—petrol, oil, man rations and dog food, to stock the depot and also to enable the ground party to continue southwards. Bad weather constantly interfered with the flying operations and heavy cloud created a major hazard because every flight had to pass through the 13,000-foot high Western Mountains. In handling the stores for the depot two of the tractor party suffered minor injuries— Peter Mulgrew broke some ribs and Murray Ellis strained his back. It was also time for Ron Balham, who was a biologist, to return to his scientific work in McMurdo Sound, so these three were evacuated to Scott Base and Ted Gawn and Derek Wright flew in as replacements. The party camped at Plateau Depot now consisted of four vehicle drivers and four dog drivers.

On 8th November the four dog teams left on the next leg of the journey south, battling against stormy winds in temperatures in the minus forties. They immediately found themselves in deep soft snow, and at this altitude they could not pull the heavily laden sledges, so a large part of the loads was left for the tractors to bring on later. On the evening of the fifth day they camped only forty-seven miles out—an average of less than ten miles a day. It was hard work.

All the necessary supplies had been flown in to Plateau Depot and on 13th November the tractors set out again, hardly able to move in their attempt to haul a load of eleven tons. They crept along for four and a half miles and then bogged down completely as the slope steepened—again they had to start relaying and in two days they had only covered thirty-five miles, while at the same time consuming large quantities of fuel. The loss of power due to the high altitude, combined with the soft snow, was proving almost too much for the Fergusons, but the Weasel was doing well and now bore the greater share of the burden, pulling five tons, while the three Fergusons roped together could manage only six tons between them. At one time their progress was so slow and their fuel consumption so high that it seemed as if their southern journey would have to come to an ignominious end, but to their relief, the surface suddenly improved when they swung on to a south-westerly heading, and the tractors gained a new lease of life.

They were now travelling on hard windblown sastrugi in thick low drift. The hard surface suited the Fergusons very well but played havoc with the heavily laden sledges, and two runners were badly damaged. The temperature was always below — 20°F, which was very cold for the drivers in their poorly protected cabs. On 19th November they passed some miles to the west of the dog teams, which had again been held up by bad weather, and pushed on ahead of them. For several days they drove in miserable weather conditions, but were encouraged because they had not encountered any major crevassed areas. But on the 24th two tractors broke through crevasse bridges and were only saved from disaster by extraordinary luck. They then found themselves in the middle of a dangerous area and retreated with a great deal of care, striking west in an attempt to find a safe way round. Soon the light became very bad and they ended the day among another group of crevasses, with two vehicles on one side of a ten-foot cavern, two on the other, and a very shaky bridge between. They decided to camp and get some sleep before trying to find their way out.

Next morning visibility had improved, and by going ahead on skis they were able to flag a route through a wide belt of crevasses. Soon they were again travelling over good surfaces and fast approaching the planned position for Depot 480, just over two hundred miles from Plateau Depot. At half-past six on 25th November they reached 79°51'S, 148°00'E, and found an area suitable for aircraft to land. Here Depot 480 was established.

Unfavourable weather prevented the Beaver from flying in the stores for the first few days, but the opportunity was taken to give the tractors an overhaul and the broken sledges were repaired. Meanwhile, to save time, a staging depot was established on the Ross Ice Shelf at the foot of the Darwin Glacier and quantities of stores were flown there, ready to be taken forward as soon as weather permitted. On the 29th John Claydon made the first flight to Depot 480, 'homing' on to the small direction-finding radio transmitter carried by the sledge party, and the build-up of the depot began.

On 28th November the dog teams had arrived. They were going much better now and had averaged sixteen miles each day during the previous week. But it was obvious that the tractors could take most of the burden of the southern journey, so in order to enable a survey to be made of the mountains around the Darwin Glacier, Ed decided to split his teams. Harry Ayres and Roy Carlyon struck east to map the large area between the

Mulock and Barne Glaciers, while, on 1st December, Bob Miller and George Marsh left with light loads to reconnoitre the route to Depot 700.

The tractors remained to receive the last loads from the aircraft. Eleven 44-gallon drums of petrol were put down, together with large quantities of food and paraffin. Murray Ellis and Peter Mulgrew had now both recovered from their injuries and rejoined the party, Ted Gawn flying back to base. On 6th December the airlift was finished and the same evening the tractors headed south.

In a determined effort to increase their daily mileage they drove for long hours, and the first two days saw them ninety-three miles farther on. But the effort proved too much for the Weasel and unpleasant grating noises in the clutch and differential made them expect the worst. The engineers were now coaxing it every inch of the way, but they had no spare parts and the end was in sight. In an effort to shed the load they established 'Midway Depot' at 81°30'S, 146°09'E, dropping six drums of fuel and thus reducing the load behind the Weasel to the caboose alone.

For ten miles they clattered through hard icy hummocks and ridges until suddenly they were in another crevassed zone and the leading tractor lurched through the first snow bridge to claw its way frantically out on the other side, leaving in its wake a gaping hole dropping away into bottomless depths. Although the crevasses were not much over four feet wide, this was enough to cause considerable concern as the vehicles crept gingerly over. Men roped together went ahead on skis to flag a route, but despite their care in selecting bridges, there was a succession of open holes by the time the last vehicle had been brought across. It took eight and a half hours to travel over this three-mile belt, and when, a few miles farther on, they struck another line of crevasses, they decided to call it a day and pitched their camp.

The engineers made a last effort to save the Weasel. The thrust bearing in the differential had disintegrated, so they made one out of brass welding rod, but despite a number of ingenious ideas for keeping it cool, it heated rapidly and proved unsatisfactory. There was nothing more they could do, so they now abandoned the Weasel, transferring additional loads to the Fergusons.

The next ninety miles were a trying experience. In the floor of every wide basin was deep, soft snow, and they were forced laboriously to 'relay' the loads across them. The hard surfaces of the ridges between were all too frequently split by crevasses, and there were many unpleasant moments. Only seven miles short of the site for Depot 700 they almost lost a tractor down a crevasse, but fortunately for the driver the crash bar over his head jammed against the wall and just held the vehicle up. On the afternoon of 15th December they covered the last few miles and rejoined Bob Miller and George Marsh, who had already established Depot 700 at 82°58′S, 146°02′E.

They were now beyond the Beaver's range from Scott Base, so the airmen put in a subsidiary depot at the foot of Shackleton Inlet, and relayed the supplies from there. The work the air contingent was carrying out with a small single-engined plane over mountain and glacier regions where the likelihood of rescue in the event of trouble was extremely remote, was beyond praise. As regularly as the weather permitted, the Beaver would appear over the horizon and touch down on the rough airstrips to unload all the necessities for the depots. Late on the afternoon of 20th December the final load arrived and the last depot was completed.

The major responsibility of the Ross Sea Party to the Crossing Party was now fulfilled, but it was only half-way through the season, and there was time for much useful work to be done. So Bob Miller and George Marsh took the two dog teams to carry out a survey of the mountains and glaciers to the west of the Beardmore Glacier, as has already been described in Chapter 8.

Ed had managed to accumulate twenty drums of fuel and was now only five hundred miles from the Pole. The tractors were still going well and he decided to push forward a further hundred miles to flag a route through another crevassed area for the benefit of our vehicle party, and then, if time allowed and no further help was required from him, attempt to drive his vehicles to the Pole itself.

At half-past eight on the evening of 20th December the party left Depot 700. They had reduced their loads to the barest minimum and were towing only six tons behind the three tractors. Their south-westerly route gave them reasonable travelling for twenty-seven miles, and they were just congratulating themselves on having by-passed all the crevasses when the leading

Ferguson broke through and barely managed to scratch its way across. This was the first of another belt of bridged crevasses and it took some hours to find a safe route through the area. All the bridges were marked with snow cairns to assist the Crossing Party later. Another thirty miles of good travelling raised their hopes once more, only to have them dashed when they entered an area of enormous crevasses. These were generally well bridged but there were several unpleasant incidents and they nearly lost the caboose when one wide bridge gave way. This proved to be their last obstacle, and once clear of the area they struck due south.

For the next six days they drove for long hours, climbing slowly to over ten thousand feet, and although the power output of the vehicles was dropping off alarmingly, as long as the surface remained reasonably firm they were able to travel slowly but steadily. On 30th December, when they were less than two hundred miles from the Pole, progress became more difficult where the surface was covered with deep soft snow. Petrol consumption increased alarmingly, and despite the light loads there were times when they had difficulty in moving at all—in one period of six hours they only travelled six miles.

Desperate measures were required if they were to get through, so they unloaded everything that could possibly be spared—food, paraffin, tractor spares, and even spare sledges were depoted, and they continued without reserves of any kind. On 2nd January they were still more than seventy miles from the Pole, and they had exactly one hundred and eighty gallons of fuel left for three vehicles. It was just enough to get them there, providing that their navigation was good and no distance was wasted in finding the Pole.

For the next twenty hours they drove steadily on, rarely exceeding three miles an hour. Every six hours Ed 'shot' the sun with his sextant to determine their position. By eight o'clock on 3rd January they had covered sixty miles and were straining their eyes for some sign of human occupation. They were stopping to refuel when Ed noticed a black dot ahead. Swerving towards it he found a marker flag. With considerable relief he signalled the others to stop and they pitched their last camp to take some much-needed sleep before pushing on. Just after midday on 4th January they drove through the last few miles of soft snow into the Pole Station. For the last time they clambered out of their cold seats and knew that their 1,250-mile journey was over.

Theirs was the first party to reach the South Pole overland since Captain Scott had done so forty-six years before. It was a great triumph for Ed Hillary and his men, who had laboured for many weeks over an unknown route with the minimum of equipment. That Ferguson tractors survived the journey over such difficult terrain was a remarkable tribute to their sturdy nature, for they had been intended only for use about the base site. But it was the faith of the men who took the risks which finally brought them to the South Pole.

11. Shackleton to the South Pole

On the other side of the continent the Crossing Party left Shackleton on the evening of 24th November 1957. The convoy was led by two Sno-Cats: first, 'Rock 'n Roll', which I shared with David Stratton; then 'Able' driven by David Pratt. Next came two Weasels: 'Rumble' and 'Wrack & Ruin', belonging to Allan Rogers and George Lowe; followed by the Muskeg tractor 'Hopalong', driven by Jon Stephenson, our Australian, who had painted a jumping kangaroo on its side. The rear was brought up by Roy Homard's Sno-Cat 'County of Kent'. Geoffrey Pratt's seismic Sno-Cat, 'Haywire', and a third Weasel were waiting for us with the dog teams at South Ice.

For many days everyone at base had been working feverishly to make ready for the start of the long journey to Scott Base. All our stores had to be sorted and packed under different headings—those items which we would take with us, things which could be flown to Halley Bay and brought home for us in the relief ship later in the season, and lastly the equipment we had to leave behind. Each Sno-Cat carried a ton of stores or equipment inside and hauled two sledges loaded with $2\frac{1}{2}$ or 3 tons each; the Weasels took half a ton inside and pulled one sledge. By far the greatest part of the total weight was fuel and oil for, with the loads they were hauling, the Sno-Cats and Weasels were each using a gallon of petrol for every $1\frac{1}{4}$ to $1\frac{1}{2}$ miles.

During the final week our little radio-room was flooded with last-minute messages of goodwill—from other Antarctic bases, from our friends and families at home, and indeed from all parts of the Commonwealth—but even so we did not then realize how much interest was being taken all over the world at the start of our journey across the continent. Ed Hillary had left Scott Base almost six weeks before and was already almost at the site of Depot 480. I now sent him a signal telling him that as we were starting ten days late and knew that the route to South Ice was difficult and dangerous, we might not be able to reach Scott Base until 9th March, but that we would do our best to make up lost time during the journey.

The R.A.F. party would remain at Shackleton to give us air cover until we travelled beyond South Ice, after which they would move up to that station themselves to prepare for their flight across the continent. On our last evening at base John Lewis prepared a special farewell feast, but loading went on well into the night and many of us did not get to bed until five o'clock in the morning of the 24th. When finally we got away it was a beautiful clear evening, the sun low on the horizon tinting the snow with delicate pastel shades of mauve, the white vapour trails from the vehicle exhausts blowing back over the sledges. We left behind John, Gordon, Peter and Taffy, who were later to fly across, and also Geoffrey Pratt who was to be flown to South Ice to carry out seismic work in that area until we arrived.

In spite of our late start we made fifteen miles before pitching camp for the night, and after fourteen miles next day we thought that we were well set for a long run. Then, as if to laugh at such optimism, a snow bridge fell away beneath Rock 'n Roll, leaving David Stratton and myself suspended in mid-air over an enormous hole—it was about fifteen feet wide and sixty feet deep to the first step in the walls of the crevasse below. Peering out of the driving seat was distinctly alarming, for I did not know how firmly the vehicle was wedged against the sides, and in any case there was nothing on to which I could step out—even the pontoons were inaccessible. However, David found that on his side he could just about reach the rear pontoon and we were able to crawl to firm snow across the ladder-like track as it hung in space over the abyss.

At first sight it looked as if we would have to abandon the vehicle—a real catastrophe at this early stage of our journey—and we began to remove everything from inside the cab. Then we determined to 'have a go' and thought out a plan to recover it. David Pratt and Roy moved the two other Sno-Cats side by side behind Rock 'n Roll and attached them by steel cables to the rear towing hook. Next, after careful prospecting along the length of the crevasse, we found a point where George and Allan could take their Weasels over and bring them round in front of Rock 'n Roll. There they were joined in tandem and attached by another cable to the Sno-Cat's front axle. In this way they formed an anchor, preventing the front of the vehicle from falling vertically into the crevasse when an attempt was made to pull it out backwards.

On a Sno-Cat each track runs round a pontoon. These pontoons are themselves free to swivel about the axles in a vertical plane, which made it very difficult for us to move the front ones into the correct position to rise over the edge of the crevasse. The Muskeg was hitched to one of the front pontoons so that it could swing it as the two Sno-Cats hauled slowly backwards. The other was helped into position by David Stratton, whom we lowered into the crevasse on a rope so that he could cut out a ledge to receive it. When everything was ready we had five vehicles to control simultaneously.

On a given signal the two Sno-Cats brought their total of 400 horse-power to bear, using the emergency low gear known to us as 'Grandma', while the Weasels kept their lines taut to hold up the front of Rock 'n Roll as she gradually moved backwards, and the Muskeg (driven in yet a third direction) brought the free pontoon safely over the edge and into position. It seemed to require a gargantuan effort and we held our breath as the vehicles strained to perform their tasks. When the recovery was at last safely accomplished, it was discovered that we had left Rock 'n Roll in forward gear all the time! The whole incident had delayed us five hours.

Next day we pressed on over many more crevasses. From our previous experience over the route we believed them to be quite small, but then we received another warning when a crevasse lid fifteen feet wide collapsed only a few feet in front of Roy's County of Kent, after all the other five vehicles had passed safely over it. When Roy stopped, his tracks were only three feet from the brink. He now had to reverse away from the hole and find another place where the crevasse could be crossed safely—a

very difficult and tedious operation as the two sledges behind him could not be pushed backwards and he could therefore only reverse a few feet at a time. After that we went ahead on skis over the route, probing for crevasses every few yards, and finding a great many which had not been there on our first journey to South Ice. Undoubtedly, during the intervening weeks, the sun had weakened the snow bridges, and now, with more vehicles to worry about, we had to be doubly careful, for we began to find monstrous black caverns beneath the seemingly smooth surface.

By the evening of the 29th we had reached the old 50-Mile Depot, but a number of minor mechanical troubles had arisen; David Pratt and Roy were constantly changing radiators, hunting for coolant leaks in the very complicated engine systems, or trying to cure obstinate ignnition troubles. We were particularly worried by the appearance of considerable wear on the rollers of Rock 'n Roll's front left track which had not been seen before she fell into the first crevasse. We were unable to find the cause (later it proved to be nothing to do with the crevasse accident), but I decided we must have a new pontoon and rollers sent out by air from Shackleton.

After leaving the depot we cleared the remaining four miles of crevasses in that particular belt and covered twenty-seven miles in the day. On 1st December we moved forty-one miles, but that night County of Kent drove into camp misfiring badly, and needing attention; we also began to dismantle the damaged pontoon on Rock 'n Roll to inspect the bearings. Maintenance work held us up until the 3rd when we travelled for thirteen hours and covered sixty-five miles over the broad undulations of the ice shelf; at the time it seemed only a fair distance, but it proved to be the best mileage we were to make until long after we had passed the South Pole.

We were now only seven miles from the eleven-mile wide crevasse belt lying in front of the ice wall, and with confidence we set out to find the chequered flag which we had planted in October to mark the first of the crevasses. As we saw it and just as I was about to say to David Stratton, 'I should stop a little way before you get there', we felt again that horrible, prolonged sinking sensation. The bonnet rose up and up in front of us, then there was a jolt and a pause, long enough to make us think we had settled, followed by a further sickening lurch as the back sank still further. Once more we were down a hole. Carefully we crept out and scrambled to the firm snow surface, where we found the front pontoons holding grimly to the other edge of the chasm while the back of the 'cat' was nearly level with the surface. When the others came up they reported that we had been breaking a number of small holes through the surface, and that they had been trying unsuccessfully to attract our attention. Here again was an area where the later season was revealing dangers we had not seen on our reconnaissance run.

As we worked to recover the vehicle it was discovered that the cause of our second lurch was the breaking of four bolts holding the towing hook, for this had torn away from the Sno-Cat and allowed the back to drop deeper. When we had Rock 'n Roll on the surface again we found that the large cast aluminium steering platform for the rear pontoons had been snapped on both sides. Fortunately David Pratt had brought a spare and repair work began at once. This went on late into the night and during the next day, while the rest of us began the endless business of probing our way through the eleven miles of crevasses—it was clear that in spite of our knowledge of the route, it was still going to be slow work.

Owing to lack of time the engineers had been unable to make three more of the complicated forward towing attachments which had been devised for Haywire on the reconnaissance journey. Therefore our three Sno-Cats could not be roped together and were in greater danger of falling into crevasses than the other vehicles. For this reason, and because the loss of a Weasel was less important than the loss of a 'cat', we now sent the two Weasels and the Muskeg ahead, roped together. In this way the leading Weasel acted as a crevasse detector.

On the 9th, we were moving forward in this new order over a section of the probed route, when David Stratton, who was ski-ing ahead to guide my leading Weasel over the prepared track, suddenly pointed back. There behind us we could see two loaded sledges but no third Sno-Cat. At first I feared that David Pratt had dropped right down a crevasse, but then I could just make out a part of the vehicle standing up in front of the sledges.

Clearly he was in a bad position and figures could be seen moving about and waving, presumably to call us back.

As we returned on skis, Hal Lister met us to say that all the vehicles would be needed for the recovery, so we unhitched from our various sledges, prodded a turning space for each vehicle, and started back over a course like a switch-back, where the numerous smaller crevasse bridges had sunk or broken through. Arriving at the scene we found Able resting in the crevasse with only the very tips of the front pontoons on the surface, the main weight of the vehicle being supported by the back of the body, and the rear pontoons hanging free.

Here was a very different recovery problem. It would be necessary to support the rear pontoons from below when the vehicle was drawn forwards, for there was certainly no possibility of hauling her out backwards. Luckily, directly beneath Able and about twenty-five feet down, the walls of the crevasse came very close together, so we all set to with shovels to fill in the hole below, until it was possible for men to stand on the snow filling we had made, and to set lengths of aluminium crevasse bridging in place beneath the pontoons. To secure them, ledges were cut into the walls of the crevasse upon which the aluminium spans could rest at a sloping angle beneath the tracks. The spans had been specially constructed in 14-foot lengths, each weighing 125 lbs. and strong enough to carry four tons.

It was impossible to put the bridging into position on both sides at exactly the same angle so the whole structure looked even more precarious than it really was. To be on the safe side steel rope slings were placed round the ends of the bridging pieces and fastened to 'dead-men', stout timbers buried several feet below the surface to act as anchors. When all was ready, Rock 'n Roll and County of Kent began to pull ahead, while two Weasels, acting as a drag anchor behind Able, gradually gave way at the back. As Able started slowly to move, the cables taut, there was suddenly a loud crunch as the ledges under the bridging gave way and the vehicle lurched sideways to sink deeper—but, to our great relief, the dead-men held. Then, like some monster rising from the deep, she seemed to heave and wallow her way to the surface, and finally came clear.

When reloading was complete, and all the tools, steel cable,

shackles, boards, bridging, ropes and other equipment had been returned to the various vehicles, we set off for the third time over the broken and sagging crevasse bridges along the trail we had already made. With a few diversions, and great care in driving, everyone reached the sledges, hooked up and continued safely to the end of the probed route.

Next day John Lewis flew out to us bringing the spare Sno-Cat pontoon and four dozen heavy steel track bars and rollers. At last, on 10th December, we cleared the crevassed area and increased our speed to a steady 8 m.p.h. until we arrived at the foot of the ice wall, after travelling for sixteen and a half hours. Expecting to encounter sunken and weakened crevasse bridges on the slope of the ice wall itself and over the wide chasms at the top, we now changed to night travel in order to take advantage of the lower temperature which would give a crisper surface, and perhaps add something to the strength of the snow bridges. Again we carefully prospected the route on skis, then slowly the vehicles clambered their ponderous way to the top. Crossing the upper crevasses with a great sense of relief we drove straight on to the Weasel which, on the reconnaissance journey, had been abandoned half a mile away.

There we dug out the sledge which had been left with it and salvaged any useful stores, while the engineers stripped the Weasel of the starter switch, the SARAH beacon, batteries and tracks. They even pumped out the anti-freeze and petrol, all of which could be useful to us. This reorganization took several hours, and I ski-ed ahead to find a new route across the great crevasse which had so alarmed us when, on the previous run to South Ice, the bridge had fallen in beside the vehicles, leaving a huge hole.

After marking out what I hoped was a safer track, I turned back to see the convoy moving slowly up the slope towards me, with Allan Rogers driving the leading Weasel, Rumble. Hal Lister was sitting on the roof acting as a look-out when suddenly Rumble slumped sideways, to be half-engulfed in the snow, and Hal was flung in a heap on the surface. Apart from torn wind-proofs and a nasty gash on his leg, he was all right, and, with the assistance of Rock 'n Roll and Wrack & Ruin, we soon had Rumble out of trouble; but the appearance of this crevasse in

what we considered to be a clear area meant that we should have to start probing again, and rather despondently we camped for the night.

Work was begun next day, everyone but the drivers ski-ing ahead in pairs to probe the track, followed by the two Weasels and the Muskeg roped together ahead of the Sno-Cats, until we reached the safer area close to the western end of the Shackleton Range. The next night we travelled thirty-one miles to reach the first zone of crevassing in the middle of the Recovery Glacier and started probing the area which had taken us five days to cross on our earlier journey. This time, aided by the markers we had left and the greater number of men to probe, we cleared the route in fourteen hours! We again found many weak places which could have spelt disaster, but at last a winding route was marked with a double row of flags. Then, with great caution, I worked Rumble gently over, with Wrack & Ruin and Hopalong keeping the safety ropes tight in case of trouble. Rather to everyone's surprise, all went well and we camped half a mile farther on with the whole of the crevassed area behind us. We had reached this point in nine days less than the time taken on our reconnaissance journey.

Again we crossed the crevasses and the high snowdrift hills encountered on the first trip, but they gave us no difficulty. Of the known trouble spots we were now faced only with the crevasses at the foot of the Whichaway Nunataks. Having marked a satisfactory route on our first journey, we expected no difficulties, but so late in the season great changes had occurred. Probing showed the area to be much worse than we had believed it to be, and as we worked slowly forward we were frequently astonished by the luck we had had on the first trip.

Continually the old tracks led across the lids of vast crevasses which could easily have swallowed all our vehicles, and twice in one day we nearly lost Ken Blaiklock. On the first occasion a bridge gave way beneath his skis, which fell eighty feet from his boots to be lost for ever, but fortunately the crevasse was narrow and he saved himself by flinging out his arms. New skis were taken to him for it would have been foolhardy to walk about on foot in such a place, and indeed a few hours later, when kneeling on them and peering into a hole he had cut in a bridge,

it suddenly fell away, leaving Ken kneeling on his skis over the middle of a four-foot wide gap! Then, last thing that night, when probing was over and we were walking to our tents beside the vehicles, the snow near my rear sledge gave way beneath Jon Stephenson and left him hanging by one elbow over a deep, dark hole from which it is doubtful if anyone could have been recovered —even if he survived the fall. It was quite a day.

We reached South Ice for the second time on 22nd December, where we joined Hannes La Grange and Geoffrey Pratt, who had been carrying on with their scientific work and caring for the dogs. When our vehicles and sledges had been parked we went to the hut for a cup of tea, but it was only built to hold four, and with twelve of us present all but the two already installed would have to sleep in tents. We were now at well over 4,000 feet and temperatures were therefore low enough for us to go back to day travel for the next part of our journey.

From South Ice we had to be self-contained for 1,100 miles— that is, until we reached Depot 700, to be laid by the Ross Sea Party working south from Scott Base. The two dog teams, driven by Ken Blaiklock and Jon Stephenson, left on 23rd December to reconnoitre the route ahead of us. They took twenty days' rations, intending to report progress by radio at eight o'clock that night, and on every date divisible by three thereafter.

With the teams away, we turned our attention to unlashing and reloading the sledges. It was certainly a busy scene, for there were now eight vehicles with twelve large sledges and a number of smaller ones. Everywhere stood piles of material: fuel barrels, jerricans, boxes, ropes and a hundred other items to be sorted, stowed and lashed down before we could be ready to leave.

When we went to our sleeping bags on Christmas Eve, 320 gallons of petrol had gone into the tanks of the eight vehicles, and the sledges carried another 109 barrels, which totalled 5,200 gallons and weighed over twenty-one tons. In addition we were taking half a ton of lubricants and one and a half tons of tools and spare parts. The remaining nine tons of our load included half a ton of explosive for the seismic work, one and a half tons of food and half a ton of paraffin for the cookers. The rest was made up of scientific equipment, tents, camping gear, ropes, skis, ice axes, and all the minor needs of a party that is to be entirely self-contained for three or four months.

At five minutes to three on Christmas afternoon all ten of us crowded into the tiny hut; bulky, padded forms filled every chair, sat on bunks and tables, or leaned against the walls to listen to the Queen's Christmas broadcast. To us, who were perhaps her most isolated audience, there seemed to be special encouragement, not only because we were proud that Her Majesty was the Expedition's Patron, but because we were engaged upon a Commonwealth enterprise.

Outside once more, there were still many last-minute things to

do. As each vehicle and its sledges were completed, the drivers decorated them with Union Jacks and Commonwealth flags; a White Ensign and the Ensign of the R.A.F. appeared, and the gay scene was enhanced by the fluttering of dozens of red and black trail pennants, together with the larger red-and-white chequered crevasse flags. Here and there coloured streamers trailed in the wind, while the low-slung Hopalong, which had been taken over by Ralph Lenton, looked more like a carnival float, decorated with a motif of tiny Chinese lanterns. As we moved off the long column was a gay, colourful sight, the vehicles winding their way round the mound that covered the deserted hut, and turning south to follow the trail pioneered by the dog teams.

Ken and Jon had already reported that they had found no trouble over the first thirty-two miles, although the surface consisted of patches of iron-hard sastrugi with areas of very soft snow lying between. At first progress was slow as the vehicles and sledges bumped and banged over the ridges, but we pushed on, to camp at the second of the six-foot cairns built by the dog party. These were made of sawn snow blocks placed one on top of the other, and stood out in the sun like shining white pillars at

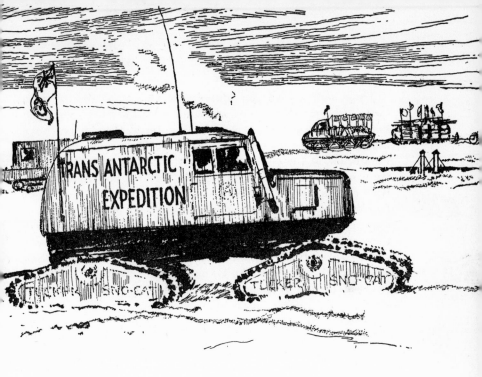

a distance of two or three miles, even against the background of the snowy surface.

At first the dog drivers were content with plain pillars, but soon they became more ambitious and we found many ingenious patterns built for our edification—and often 'Monopoly' messages such as 'If you throw a six you can jump this one' or, 'Go South, young man'. But their pride was the two-pillared cairn with a cross-piece, labelled 'SNOWHENGE'.

Next day whiteout prevented us from moving without serious risk to the convoy, but by the evening the sky was clearing and we drove off over more hard and extensive sastrugi. That night we stopped at the dog party's 35-mile cairn. There had been trouble with coolant leaks on Hal Lister's Weasel, and David Pratt in Able was keeping him company. When the time came to camp there was no sign of either of them. Next morning they had still not appeared, so Roy Homard and Allan Rogers went back in Hopalong, which could travel quickly and easily over the sastrugi. Meanwhile, Geoffrey Pratt and Hannes La Grange went ahead with Haywire to complete the next seismic station thirty miles on, so that we should not be held up by that particular task when we got on the move again.

These seismic shots for sounding the depth of the ice were quite a complicated process and altogether the work took some hours to carry out. As we made the observations every thirty miles, we were very often held up until Geoffrey had finished. First of all, at the end of twelve or thirteen hours of travelling, we would pitch the tents, then begin boring a hole three inches wide and thirty-six feet deep. This would take three men about two hours. At the same time, others would lay out 330 metres of electric cable to which we connected forty-eight geophones; these were the receivers of shock waves reflected from the rock surface below the ice when a charge of ten pounds of explosive was fired electrically at the bottom of the borehole. The waves received by the geophones were electrically transmitted to a photographic recorder in Haywire and from the time taken for the shock to travel down through the ice, 'bounce' off the rock underneath and come back to the surface, we could calculate the depth of the ice at that point. Before we packed up the equipment the photographic record was always developed to make sure that we had a result. On the few occasions when the 'shot' was a failure, a second was fired before we moved on.

As all Geoffrey's instruments were very sensitive to any sort of vibration, it was essential that during the firing we should all remain absolutely still. On his Sno-Cat Geoffrey carried a large and very loud ship's bell which was always rung as a warning to everyone to stop whatever they were doing and keep quiet just before the shot went off.

The seismic borehole would be drilled last thing at night and then filled with clusters of Hal Lister's glaciological thermometers at different depths. In the morning Hal would have much useful data for his particular work and the 'shot' would then be fired in the hole just before we were ready to move off on the day's run.

At last, just before nine o'clock, Hopalong, Able, and Hal's Weasel pulled into camp; a new radiator had had to be fitted to the Weasel. We set off at twenty-past ten that night and had travelled fifteen miles by a quarter-to four in the morning when we camped at the 55-mile cairn. So developed the picture of events which was to be our lot throughout almost the entire journey; long hours slowly grinding over hard sastrugi or through deep soft snow, frequent minor troubles with vehicles, time

156

spent every three hours in taking meteorological and gravity observations, and the periodic boring of holes for seismic shooting. Camping, eating, vehicle maintenance and sleeping had all to be fitted into what few hours remained. As a result there was generally very little time for sleep and at the end of the journey we all felt that our worst hardship had been the lack of proper rest.

On 29th December we reached 83°33′S, 29°02′W, and an approximate altitude of 5,800 feet. Here we caught up with the dog teams, just a hundred miles from South Ice. General vehicle maintenance, carried out every two hundred miles, was now due, and a number of sledge towbars which had been broken by the heavy going had to be electrically welded. Our stop was therefore longer than usual and the dogs went ahead again. The increasing altitude was making the Sno-Cats overheat as they hauled their six-ton load in second and third gears, and I took the opportunity of replacing the four-bladed fan on Rock 'n Roll with another having six blades. This effectively cured the trouble, and later the fans on the other 'cats' were also changed.

On New Year's Eve troubles came one after another. Welding of more towbars took much longer than we expected, there were difficulties with two Weasels, and when we were finally about to start at seven in the evening, Hal's rammsonde became stuck three metres down in the snow and we had to dig a pit to that depth before we could recover it.

A rammsonde instrument is used to measure the density of the various snow layers beneath the surface. It consists of a graduated tube ending in a conical shaped piece of metal which is driven into the snow by a succession of blows. As each metre of tube is driven down, another metre's length is screwed to the top and the process continued. The blows are delivered by a piece of metal of known weight which is allowed to slide down a rod and strike the top of the tube from a known height. This means that the force of each blow is known. By observing the distance to which the tube and cone are driven into the snow by, say, five blows, the resistance of the snow can be recorded. As the instrument sinks down one finds that there is great variation in this resistance; sometimes five blows will drive it in, say, ten centimetres, while it takes ten blows for it to go down the next two centimetres.

These differences in density below the surface represent changes of weather conditions during the time that the mass of snow accumulated, and much can be learnt by such a study.

At half-past eight, the rammsonde recovered, we at last moved off, but did not get very far. First, George Lowe broke a sledge runner, and then Allan Rogers's Rumble broke a track and had to be abandoned as we had no replacement. It was planned that vehicles would be left behind as the fuel they hauled was used up, and six miles back we had said goodbye to the Muskeg, Hopalong, the first to go. Now we went back and picked it up to replace Rumble. As a result of all these troubles we camped where we were and saw in the New Year at midnight with a single tot of whisky for each man which we had carried for the occasion.

Next day conditions were good and we hoped to cover fifty miles, but the surface was too soft for Hopalong, which was towing two heavy sledges, and she could not travel faster than two to three miles per hour. Everyone had a soft spot for Hopalong because she had gone so far and so well with a heavy load and given no trouble. When first we had left her we had all been sad, then delighted when she had joined us again, but having no Muskeg spares we knew she would have to be the next to go. To speed our progress the second sledge was now taken from her and put as a third behind County of Kent. The Muskeg could now keep up 5 m.p.h. in third gear—she had never been in top gear the entire 530 miles from Shackleton. In all we covered thirty-nine miles that New Year's Day, the last nine over bad sastrugi which, in the end, so separated the vehicles that we were forced to camp to let them assemble. In my journal I wrote:

Another 30 miles today, but what a labour! All vehicles in first and second gear all the day over the most corrugated fields of continuous sastrugi. The strain on vehicles and sledges is prodigious; particularly I worry about the gear-boxes, for the constant hours of heavy work in low gear are bound to tell on them. Already Rock 'n Roll's lay-shaft is very much noisier than it was. One bright spot is that the six-bladed fan now maintains the engine at 160°F, even with the radiator doors half shut.

With the dog tracks still guiding us there was no need for navigation. Haywire continued ahead of us with seismic work, followed by the two Weasels and the Muskeg which were slower than the 'cats' over the murderous sastrugi. It was impossible to go round the high iron-hard ridges, for they formed a great field that extended as far as we could see. Each driver had to judge the course for his own particular type of vehicle, and often we found ourselves scattered a mile or two apart, working and weaving our way among ridges four or five feet high. Sometimes vehicles and sledges had very deliberately to be driven at a speed of half a mile an hour or less over vertical drops. Twisting and turning, sometimes at right angles to our course, we tried to keep within reasonable distance of the dog sledge tracks which preserved a fairly steady line and prevented us from making too much extra mileage. Here and there even the dog team trail wandered and the tracks in the snow revealed the upsetting of a sledge; where two ski tracks ended abruptly against a ridge we knew that some-one had come to grief.

Mile after mile this trial of tempers and equipment continued. All day on 3rd January we travelled over the most vicious sastrugi. More and more towbars were damaged, so that most of the towing was by steel rope, which was very hard on the trans-missions because there is no spring in steel cable and as the sledges slid forward down slopes, catching up the tractors, then slowed up or stopped at the next rise, the cable would sud-denly snap taut. The shock was transmitted from the vehicle through the tracks to axles, drive shafts, differentials, gears and clutch.

On 2nd January we caught up with the dog teams again and they travelled with us. By now we had taken to using a sun compass, for the magnetic compass was already becoming sluggish as we travelled nearer to the South Magnetic Pole. We had mounted a pair of these instruments, one on either side of Rock 'n Roll, and when the sun was cut off from the driver's instrument by the shadow of the vehicle, the co-driver would call out the heading from the compass on the other side. As the altitude increased the amount of oxygen available in a given volume of air decreased and we had therefore to change the carburettor jets on all the vehicles every two thousand feet above the 4,000-

foot line so as to keep the mixture of air and fuel correct. This could not increase the power of the engines but was a considerable economy measure.

It was at this time that Ed Hillary sent me a message suggesting that as it was already getting late in the season, we should stop at the South Pole and ask the Americans to fly us out to Scott Base. This rather surprised us as we were already moving more quickly and had gained great confidence in our vehicles. I therefore replied that we would continue as planned. Ed of course had himself arrived at the South Pole with his three companions on 4th January and he stayed there for a few days before being flown back to Scott Base in an American aircraft. In view of the soft surfaces which he reported just the other side of the Pole, which would cause our Sno-Cats to use more fuel, I now asked him to fly in additional supplies to Depot 700.

At last, on 5th January, we passed out of the sastrugi belt and thankfully drove thirty-two miles in the day. It was a tremendous relief to be able to travel two or three consecutive miles in top gear, for up till now the vehicles had ground along in low gears almost the whole way from Shackleton. In 575 miles we had driven perhaps forty-five miles in 'top'.

The time had come to abandon our second vehicle and again we regretfully prepared to say goodbye to Hopalong. It also meant leaving one of the large sledges which could no longer be towed. This, with fourteen empty fuel drums, formed a memorial pile to the Muskeg, a hard working and still active friend whose life ended in latitude 85°15′S.

Two days later we were making better progress, covering about thirty miles a day—which was as much as the dogs could manage—but we found a broken 'U' bolt on Hal's Weasel, while Wrack & Ruin was burning a pint of oil every five miles with a petrol consumption of one and a half miles to the gallon. Soon we should have to decide which would be the next to go. Slowly the days passed, and each evening now we were about thirty miles nearer the Pole.

The scientific work was uninterrupted. Every three hours Hannes made his meteorological observations and Geoffrey made a gravity observation. Hal was constantly observing the snow conditions and at any lengthy halt made a rammsonde measurement. The end of each day found us boring the 36-foot hole for the seismic sounding next morning.

On 13th January we were again in another belt of sastrugi ten miles wide when both the dog drivers, Ken and Jon, had to stop with severe stomach troubles and temperatures. We quickly pitched their tent and made them as comfortable as possible in their sleeping bags. Roy Homard, Hal Lister, George Lowe and David Pratt had all suffered the same trouble in varying degrees and it seemed that some infection was running through the party. For the next two days the dogs were driven by David Stratton and George Lowe to give our invalids a chance to recover.

It was in latitude 88°03′S that we abandoned Hal's Weasel. By now it had four broken 'U' bolts and was leaking oil in ever increasing quantities. The glaciological equipment was transferred to Rock 'n Roll in which Hal was to travel with David Stratton and me for the remainder of the journey.

On the morning of 17th January we were camped at 88°45′S— eighty-five miles from the Pole—when two American planes flew over while we were still in our sleeping bags. Ralph Lenton scrambled up to speak to them from the County of Kent radio and heard that they were carrying Ed Hillary, John Lewis and Admiral Dufek, the commander of the United States 'Deepfreeze' Operations. John had by now flown from South Ice to Scott Base —the story of the flight is told in the next chapter.

On 19th January we began our last run before reaching the Pole—over a soft and smooth surface. And then we saw it! At the top of a snow ridge we halted to climb on top of our vehicles and scan the horizon with binoculars for the markers we had been told to expect. Suddenly a cluster of huts and radio masts sprang into the field of vision. They seemed only a short distance away (about seven miles), but the Chief Scientific Officer of the American Pole Station had particularly asked us to avoid the snow areas which they were studying and to come in along the 24°W meridian; so we turned along the top of the ridge until we found the line of flags which showed us the route they wished us to use. The following extract from my journal describes our arrival:

Today we have run in to the Pole, the distance being 32 miles instead of only 26 as we expected, because when we

sighted the Pole Station we were too far west in longitude
and they had asked us to come in on meridian 24°W to avoid
the snow areas being studied. It took us some time, and
seven miles to find the barrel and line of flags which marked
the route in. When the Pole Station came into view it was
about seven miles distant and though apparently on a ridge
there was a hollow between us and it.

By the time we had turned south along the line of flags,
the dogs were tiring, and the convoy moved slowly so that
they could keep up and arrive together with the vehicles.
The day was a brilliant one, without a cloud, and only a
light wind from about the 80°E meridian. As the party
moved towards the Pole, I looked back and thought our
convoy a brave sight; the orange 'cats' and Weasel, together
with the loaded sledges, bearing many fluttering flags of
different colours. Besides the national Commonwealth flags,
there was that of the city of Bristol, a TAE flag embroidered
by Ralph, chequered crevasse flags, trail pennants, and a
special green one embroidered by Hannes with a springbok
on one side, and a protea on the other. Above all this the great
condensation plumes streamed away from the high, open
exhausts of the Sno-Cats.

Ahead of us we could see two Weasels moving out
towards us from the station, but they stopped two miles before
meeting us. As we approached nearer, we could see quite a
crowd, in fact over 30 people all armed with cameras.
These included Admiral Dufek, Ed Hillary, Griff Pugh,
Peter Mulgrew, the reporters and all the base personnel.
Among the latter were Lieutenant Verne Houk, United
States Navy Medical Service in administrative control of the
base, and Major Mogesson ('Mogy') in charge of the scientific
work.

On jumping out of the 'cat' I first shook hands with Ed,
then George Dufek and the base leaders. There was such a
press of photographers and recorders that it was quite
difficult to move about. After the first 'milling' had sub-
sided, Houk and Dufek climbed into my 'cat' and I drove
them on to the base where Houk directed me to the parking
site.

The next move was to wash and have a meal, followed by a press conference and a radio recording for the BBC through McMurdo Sound.

Our reception has been a most warm one and we have been invited to sleep and eat in the base instead of our tents. This makes our stay here pleasant, informal and a complete rest.

As we had not crossed the 'date line', our day was still the 19th, but we find the Americans are keeping NZ time, which makes it 20th January. Their actual time is GMT plus twelve hours. We therefore arrived in our night and their midday. I decided we should change over to their time at once by treating our night as day, and going to bed early if individuals wished. In fact, I think most of us have missed a complete night's sleep.

The Crossing Party had reached the South Pole by the over-land route. First Amundsen with his dog teams, so closely followed by the gallant but doomed Scott on foot, then Ed with his strange assortment of vehicles, and now our own convoy. But while the newspapers of the world headlined our arrival there, we knew that it was only the half-way mark, and that much travel and work lay ahead of us before we ourselves could consider that our task had been successfully accomplished.

12. The Trans-Polar flight

While we were still on our way from South Ice to the Pole, the R.A.F. contingent had the task of closing down Shackleton. It was planned that they should then fly across the continent to Scott Base, there joining the Beaver and providing air support in the later stages of our journey. This would be the first trans-Antarctic flight ever attempted in a small single-engined aircraft. This chapter tells the story of their successful achievement.

The Royal Society Expedition had kindly offered to send back to England in their relief ship, our Auster aircraft and any equipment, scientific specimens or records we could deliver to Halley Bay. Accordingly, the R.A.F. party, John Lewis, Gordon Haslop, Peter Weston and Taffy Williams, who were left behind at Shackleton while we struggled laboriously to South Ice for the second time, spent long hours in sorting and packing stores.

On 9th December, Operation 'Pickford' got under way, and John and Gordon flew the planes to Halley Bay, taking Peter to dismantle and prepare the Auster for shipment when the relief ship arrived. Taffy remained at base to maintain our radio communications. In four days the Otter was back and they began the task of closing down Shackleton. Water tanks were drained, windows boarded up, chimneys plugged and the hut swept clean.

A single-engined plane cannot afford mechanical breakdowns over the inhospitable Antarctic continent, so now Peter thoroughly overhauled the Otter before her long flight, fitting the auxiliary tank in the fuselage which would double her endurance. The total of 356 gallons of fuel gave a flying range, in still air, of 1,600 miles. The distance from South Ice to Scott Base was 1,450 miles—so there was a bare margin of 150 miles for errors in navigation or strong headwinds.

The party mustered their emergency gear, tents, forty days' food (combining the normal sledging ration with the R.A.F. survival rations on which Gordon had already lived on the ice shelf), pots and pans, Primus stoves, sleeping bags, shovels, ice axes, ropes—all these had to be assembled.

Now came the problem of weight. The maximum load of the Otter was one ton, although in fact our pilots had always operated at or just above this limit. Now, with the auxiliary tank fitted, a very large proportion of the load was taken up with fuel, while the four men, fully dressed in bulky cold-weather flying kit, weighed 1,000 lbs. between them. Each ounce counted, and all the rations and equipment were removed from their metal or wooden containers and repacked in polythene bags to save weight; every item was then weighed before going into the plane.

We had left South Ice on Christmas Day, and now that we were fifty miles on our way towards the Pole and no longer needed the Otter, they could move up to South Ice and wait for suitable weather conditions to cross to Scott Base. After lunch on 27th December they were ready, and, as they had loaded the plane exactly as they would when finally leaving South Ice, the take-off provided useful experience for their final departure. But Shackleton was only two hundred feet above sea level, and there would still be some anxiety about getting the overladen machine safely off the ground in the thinner air at an altitude of 4,430 feet.

The temperature had risen to 15°F, which made the surface tacky, and there was almost no wind as the aircraft started its run. An anxious moment as the Otter slowly gathered speed across the snow, and then the tail came up—in five hundred yards they were airborne. After two or three circuits round the now-deserted Shackleton base, which would soon become obliterated by the drifting snow, they set course for South Ice.

It was a beautiful, sunny day with a gentle breeze—perfect flying weather—and this short trip provided the opportunity for checking the aircraft itself, the navigational equipment, and the radio, under actual flying conditions. Although the aircraft had been equipped with special instruments to assist navigation in this difficult area, it was still a great problem to maintain a true course over the featureless ice cap. In more populated areas, long-distance flights are guided by numerous radio stations and weather reports which were not available here.

The flight to South Ice was free from incident, and took just under three hours, the Otter landing at five o'clock in the afternoon. While the pilots and Peter Weston at once began to unload the sleeping bags, refuel the plane and prepare a meal, Taffy was keeping radio schedules, first with us and then with the American Pole Station. Some time before, the American radio operators had agreed to a daily contact at seven o'clock each evening, when they would pass the weather report from Scott Base together with their own forecasts of the weather at the Pole. From our vehicle party's normal schedule at six o'clock Taffy would hear of intermediate weather conditions, and piecing together the three messages, they would have some idea of conditions over the whole extent of their flight. The only 'catch' was that the weather reports from Scott Base would already be twelve hours old, and conditions in the Antarctic can change abruptly in far less time than that.

Taffy was also in daily radio communication with Halley Bay, which was now the link with our London headquarters, and told them that the Otter was standing by ready to fly, awaiting a suitable day. On the evening of the 28th the forecast along the route was bad; in our area it was cloudy with slight snow, and the flight was out of the question. On the 29th they spent a long day under cloudless skies, waiting for the evening 'sked', but at six o'clock when Taffy came up on the air, he could get no response from us owing to bad radio conditions. The four of them sat for another hour around the radio set, waiting impatiently until the Pole Station broadcast—if indeed it was able to get through. Punctually on the hour contact was made, and they learnt that some patches of cloud were expected over the Pole and thin, layered cloud at Scott Base. It was not ideal, but it could have been worse. They decided to have a go, and asked the Pole Station to inform Scott Base that they would be leaving.

It had always been planned that they would start from South Ice in the late evening, thus ensuring that throughout the estimated twelve hours of their flight they would have the sun ahead of them, making it unnecessary to circuit the aircraft to take a sun-sight and thus use up valuable fuel. Now bedding was hastily rolled up, kit packed, the Thermos flasks filled and the aircraft given a last check. Gordon was to be the pilot, while John navigated, and he opened the throttle, waggling the rudder to free the skis from the tacky snow. This was their most worrying moment—would the heavily laden plane take off at this altitude from a surface made sticky by the blazing sun, and without any helping wind? The Otter jolted forward, slowly at first, then gradually accelerating, and the tail came up. The speed crept up to 55 knots, Gordon eased down the flaps to take-off position, the plane bounced twice as if to gather strength— and then she was airborne. Four deep sighs of relief were clearly audible. It had taken a run of well over half a mile to get the small plane off the ground. The time was 10.27 p.m. and the sun still shone brightly.

They circled the tiny speck that was the South Ice station for a last look, and then set course along the 29°W meridian for the Pole, 550 miles and five hours' flying time away. The Otter climbed slowly at a constant speed, gaining height as the fuel was used up and the plane lightened. The Pole itself lies at an altitude of something under 10,000 feet, and on the far side they would have to cross country known to rise to 11,000 feet. Even if they could coax the aircraft up to 12,000 feet, the margin of clearance was very fine.

For the first hour all went well, and the sight of the vehicle party camped below them two miles to port confirmed the accuracy of their navigation. Taffy called up on the radio, but we had had a long day and Ralph Lenton was tucked up, oblivious to the aircraft, in his sleeping bag. They gained a little more height and flew on for another ninety miles when they could see clouds on the far horizon. At 1.52 a.m. on the 30th the Otter was flying above a thin layer of stratus and conditions were deteriorating. Ahead the cloud was thicker, and half an hour later they were in a dense mass which appeared to rise to at least 14,000 feet. The aircraft was now flying at 10,000 feet and the rate of climb was very slow, while the surface below was at 8,000 feet and the country ahead invisible and unknown.

One of the objects of this flight was to provide us with a report on the surfaces we could expect between latitude 84°S and the Pole. It was thought that a range of mountains, or at least a disturbance of the surface where they were submerged by the ice, might cross our route, and if so, some idea of its extent and the difficulties it might present would be invaluable; but at two o'clock they were still flying in thick cloud at 87°40′S, and sticky rime ice began to form along the leading edges of the wings, causing the Otter to lose height dangerously. Cloud still enveloped them, and the risk of flying on in the hope that the weather might improve was becoming too much of a gamble. They held a brief consultation and very reluctantly decided that they must return to South Ice.

Their problem was now reversed. If it was too hazardous to fly to a spot on the map about a thousand miles ahead, it was almost as difficult to turn back four hundred miles and pinpoint a small black dot in the middle of miles and miles of nothing after a seven-hour flight. The best hope was that the Whichaway Nunataks and the Shackleton Mountains, lying to the north of South Ice, would act as signposts to the deserted station. John Lewis took over the aircraft, and at 2.45 a.m. the Otter came out of the cloud and flew steadily northwards for nearly two hours. Then four big smiles broke out simultaneously —for dead ahead, their white-plumed vapour trails streaming out behind them, the vehicle party had come into view! But their anxieties were not yet over.

At five o'clock an ominously dark patch stretched across their path—thick stratus cloud that had moved in from the north. As the aircraft approached the clearly defined edge, they saw that it extended right down to the surface—now what should they do? John lost height but soon realized that he would be flying blind once he entered the murk. They circled round and discussed the next move. Suddenly, immediately below them, they spotted vehicle tracks in the snow. From the outward flight they remembered that except for one 'jink' these led in a straight line from South Ice—and the 'jink' was only about a quarter of a mile from the station. 'Flying by Bradshaw' or finding one's bearings by following railway lines has brought many a plane safely home, and John gratefully accepted the present chance. Without more ado he descended to only ten feet above the ground and skimmed along the 'railway lines' for forty miles towards South Ice. The visibility was about a hundred yards, but where the tracks jinked sharply right, he closed the throttle, lowered the flaps and touched down, coming to rest not ten yards from the spot where the Otter had taken off over seven hours earlier!

The four men climbed out, frustrated at being back at their starting point; the aircraft was picketed and the sleeping bags moved back into the hut. After a hot drink they were glad to go to bed, and slept until late in the afternoon of New Year's Eve. Then once again they anxiously awaited the weather reports. On the surface a twenty-knot wind was blowing, whipping up thick drift and snow. The day was overcast and bitterly cold; this was not flying weather—indeed, in these conditions, they could not even refuel the Otter. So, with a clear conscience they settled down to welcome the New Year in with a four-course dinner of soup, fishcakes, stew and fruit, followed by coffee. They drank to the Queen, the vehicle party, and to themselves—and went to bed to wait for another day and to hope that the storm would blow itself out.

But for the next three days the high winds continued. They chafed at the delay, and it was little consolation to hear that conditions at Scott Base were just as bad. On 4th January the wind died down and conditions improved enough for the aircraft to be refuelled and for Peter Weston to check it over.

When the complete stock of fuel had been emptied into the tanks the Otter was still short of twenty-five gallons, enough for one hour's flying time. The safety margin, narrow enough in the first place, was now non-existent. Four 40-gallon drums of aviation fuel, all that remained of the original 9,000 gallons we had brought down in the *Magga Dan*, had been left behind at Shackleton when the base was evacuated. On the radio Taffy was speaking to the American station called Ellsworth, which was only fifty miles along the coast from Shackleton. Hearing of the situation the base commander suggested that the Ellsworth plane should call at Shackleton, pick up this fuel and bring it to

South Ice. This generous offer was gratefully accepted, and early on 6th January the drums were delivered and the Otter topped up.

The weather had cleared and at last it looked as though they might be able to try again. Hoping that the forecast that evening would be favourable, they loaded the plane and again made ready.

During their six o'clock schedule with us we were able to tell them that we were travelling under clear skies with hardly any wind and good visibility. An hour later they were talking to the Pole Station, where the forecast was equally good, and Taffy passed the message that the Otter would take off at about half-past eleven and was expected to take twelve hours to reach Scott Base.

Once more they were feverishly busy. All the emergency gear was re-checked, Thermos flasks filled once more and the aircraft skis dug out of the drifted snow. Luckily a light breeze was blowing and the lower air temperature had improved the surface. At 11.48 p.m., and this time with a shorter run, the Otter was again airborne.

Course was set, and speaking to the Pole Station Taffy arranged to call them every thirty minutes until they reached the head of the Beardmore Glacier—after which Scott Base would take over radio control. The plane climbed slowly but steadily and just over two hours later they sighted our vehicles three miles to port. Taffy tried to make contact, but once more Ralph was asleep, as we had not heard from the Pole Station that they would definitely fly that night, and Taffy's greetings fell on deaf ears.

A following wind was helping them to eke out their fuel, and by four o'clock eager eyes were straining ahead for the first glimpse of the Pole, which they hoped to reach half an hour later. But now the surface became obscured by ice crystals which formed a thick haze, not unlike the smog patch that hangs over industrial towns. At 4.23 a.m. the Otter's loop aerial picked up the transmissions from the beacon at the Pole, and five minutes later the station buildings appeared through the haze immediately below them. The Stars and Stripes and the United Nations flag marked the Pole itself, and circling round and round, 'flying' as John put it, 'out of Tuesday, into Wednesday and back again to Tuesday', they talked to the Americans below.

Gordon, a staunch New Zealander, was delighted to be 'in the right quadrant of the globe' once more, and received Maori greetings from his fellow Kiwis at Scott Base before the aircraft set course for the Beardmore Glacier.

They had completed the first leg of their journey and their route was now almost identical with that taken by Captain Scott forty-seven years before. All being well, they would cover in a few hours the tragic route that he and his companions had trudged with such brave effort over so many weeks.

An hour and forty minutes later a line of mountains came up to starboard and was identified as the Dominion Range. Now the landmarks were coming into focus and ahead on the horizon they could pick out the peaks of the Queen Alexandra Range. At seven o'clock they were over the head of the Beardmore Glacier and marvelled at this strange river of ice that wound down eight thousand feet, between formidable mountains, to the Ross Barrier nearly a hundred and fifty miles away.

Our people at home had been anxious about this flight, and remembering that messages from the London office were always signed 'Transpolar', which was their telegraphic address, John now sent an exuberant message to headquarters giving his position and ending 'Downhill all the way. Viva Transpolar.'

In clear skies and brilliant sunshine they lost height and enjoyed the magnificent scenery as they flew down the glacier. To port a mountain called the Cloudmaker lived up to its name, wearing a small cloud like a delicate white halo round its summit, and then they could see Mount Hope and the Ross Barrier, which stretched to the horizon like a huge frozen lake.

Now friendly voices were coming over the air, and Scott Base was preparing its reception. The aircraft droned on—every minute bringing it nearer to the end of a unique flight, and tail winds caused them to advance their time of arrival to eleven o'clock. Passing the message, Taffy took the opportunity of ordering 'four bottles of very cold beer'. At half-past nine Mount Discovery jutted out of the slight haze and then the low, dark line of Minna Bluff came into view. They were nearly there. Passing the end of the Bluff, the plane crossed between Black and White Islands, and then Ross Island loomed up ahead, with its twin volcanic peaks, Mount Erebus and Mount Terror.

Here they were met by an aerial reception committee. Two United States Navy Otters, from the American base at McMurdo Sound, flew out to greet them, both crammed with Americans and New Zealanders, packed, as Gordon described it, 'like quills on a porcupine, and every one of them with a camera trained on us'.

The escorting planes took station on either side of them as they approached Scott Base. Ted Gawn, the base radio operator, could not bear to miss the party when they landed and so, excitedly shouting, 'There you are. You can see the landing strip now. I'm off to be there when you get down,' he abruptly went off the air and raced for the runway.

As they circled the base, more American aircraft—Dakotas and Otters—came up to meet them and described exuberant circuits of welcome. The Otter went down, with the two American planes flying slightly ahead on either side to guide it in. Then, almost from ground level, whilst it triumphantly touched down, the escorting aircraft roared upwards to join their compatriots in the air—much to the chagrin of all the enthusiastic photographers now borne out of range!

After a flight of exactly eleven hours and 1,430 statute miles, our little single-engined aircraft had made it. As the party clambered stiffly out they were engulfed by a friendly crowd of Americans and New Zealanders, for everyone in McMurdo Sound was there to greet them. Ed Hillary, who had himself only just flown back from the Pole, led the congratulations, and there was a special welcome from John Claydon and Bill Cranfield, the two New Zealand pilots, who could perhaps best appreciate the problems of their flight.

A happy touch was the story of 'Taffy's Tankard'. During the winter months at Shackleton, our regular radio schedules with the Pole Station had created a firm friendship between the American radio operators and Taffy and Ralph. Knowing that one of the Americans was due for relief, there was constant chit-chat, and some betting as to whether he or Taffy would reach McMurdo Sound first. It had been agreed that whichever did would greet the other with a glass of beer. Now, as our four airmen were lined up to be photographed from every angle, a stranger, carefully nursing a tankard, stepped out of the crowd and handed it to Taffy. A promise had been kept!

13. The South Pole to Scott Base

We received a wonderful welcome from the hospitable Americans at the Pole Station. They gave a party in our honour at which each of us was presented with a splendid testimonial certifying that we had 'been round the world on our feet'—an awesome sounding journey which merely entailed walking once round the flagstaff marking the Pole itself.

In turn, we presented the Station with the Expedition pennant to commemorate our visit, and showed them the signed portrait of Her Majesty the Queen which had hung at Shackleton and which we had determined to carry across the continent. We also unfurled the flag of the Scottish National Antarctic Expedition, 1901–3, taken south by William Spears Bruce on his voyage in the *Scotia*, when he had discovered Coats Land, on the east side of the Weddell Sea. This had been handed to me in Edinburgh by the President of the Royal Scottish Geographical Society with the request that we should take it across Antarctica with us. Our hosts were also deeply interested in Captain Scott's watch, taken by him to the Pole on his last journey, which I had worn on a leather thong round my neck since we left Shackleton. Smith's of Cricklewood had taken it from their museum and entrusted it to me to take back to the Pole and on to Scott Base. (It has now been returned to the museum, where it can be seen on display.)

But the four days we spent at the Pole were also very busy ones, for there was much to do. First, our sledge loads had to be unlashed, empty fuel barrels discarded, and all our stores repacked on to fewer sledges, for we intended lightening our loads as much as possible. No fuel or stores were taken on at the Pole—except for a case of jam presented to us to vary our rather dull trail rations.

Our electric welder was set up on Haywire, which had been taken into the Station workshop, and there work went ahead repairing the broken towbars and mending and modifying our battery heating equipment, for it would be disastrous if, with the approaching end of the season and the lower daily temperatures, the batteries froze and the Sno-Cats had no electrical power.

Hal Lister, Hannes La Grange, Allan Rogers and Geoffrey Pratt all had their own scientific work to do, and spent long periods in discussion with their opposite numbers of the American staff. When Haywire was at last released from her welding duties in the Station workshop, Geoffrey set off in her to make his scheduled seismic shot. It was some time—and a number of shots—before he had a satisfactory result, because the strong wind interfered with the recording of his sensitive geophones, but eventually his apparatus showed the ice to be nearly eight thousand feet thick, an increase of over five thousand feet in the last twenty-five miles, indicating the presence of an ice-buried mountain range in the vicinity.

It was five o'clock on 24th January when we were ready to go and to say goodbye to our American friends. Exactly two months before we had left Shackleton, some 950 miles away—now it was another 1,250 to Scott Base, but we could expect to move more quickly because we had fewer vehicles to maintain, the seismic soundings would be spaced more widely and Ed Hillary had pioneered a route which we could follow. Also, from a safety point of view, once we reached Depot 700 we should be within range of the Beaver and the Otter.

We did not expect temperatures below −40°F until well into March, and as we had already operated our vehicles down to −60°F and knew that we could endure temperatures as low as that in tents, uncomfortable though it might be, our only real concern was the possible persistence of strong winds and drift or long periods of whiteout which could certainly delay us seriously. If an early freeze-up in McMurdo Sound forced H.M.N.Z.S. *Endeavour* to leave, we should be committed to another winter in the Antarctic, but this was a risk we had recognized even before we left England, and supplies for an extra year had been ordered for both Shackleton and Scott Base.

We drove away from the Pole Station along the 156°E meridian into light but high drift. Passing the ring of barrels and the two flagstaffs marking the Pole itself, we motored slowly round in a close circle; in the two minutes it took to do this we had passed through twenty-four hours of time and returned to the present, while every point on earth had been due north of us.

The Magnetic Pole was still 1,250 miles away and it was confusing to find that as we turned north on to our course, the compasses still showed us travelling south, so when driving it was necessary to remember that any diversion to the east was really to the west!

For the first eighteen miles the Americans had planted small trail flags every tenth of a mile so that we could follow the same route they used and not plough great ruts across the virgin snow areas which they were studying. At a pile of fuel drums marking the end of the line we altered course to bring us over to the 140°E meridian which we intended to follow so as to pick up the tracks of Ed Hillary's vehicles. When we stopped at midnight we had covered twenty-five miles and had climbed about a hundred and thirty feet above the Pole Station. By now the increased altitude had reduced the power of our engines to about half the sea level output of 200 h.p., and our fuel consumption was up to 0·9 miles per gallon—for all five vehicles this worked out at about two tons of petrol for a hundred miles.

Next morning the seismic shot showed the depth of ice to be less than two thousand feet, which showed that we had again reached a high rock area covered by a relatively thin mantle of ice. It therefore seems that the Geographical South Pole is situated above a great ice-filled basin some fifty miles wide and lying between two rocky ranges that are themselves completely hidden by the ice.

On the 25th and 26th we ran thirty-five and forty miles respectively in strong winds and some drift, and on the following day found the sledges, food, paraffin, bottles of gas for welding, tarpaulins, old tents and other unwanted items which Ed had left behind when the soft snow had held up his tractors. We camped after forty-two miles, and by the time we had bored the hole for the next morning's seismic shot, and Hal had established his thermometers in it, it was nearly four o'clock in the morning —but we had long since resigned ourselves to late hours and always tried to gain sleeping time in the Sno-Cats when not actually driving.

Next morning preparations for the shot began as usual; the bell rang, but at the critical moment the charge failed to explode. I was puzzled to see David Stratton come running across to me, his face betraying some anxiety. He had found Geoffrey Pratt lying unconscious on the floor of Haywire, with his eyes closed and his limbs twitching. Quickly he had fetched Allan Rogers, who immediately diagnosed carbon-monoxide poisoning; while Allan improvised a crude face mask from a handkerchief, a wild scramble took place to find the welding oxygen. Geoffrey was given sufficient to bring him round, and we then carried him over to his tent and made him as comfortable as possible.

He was in a serious condition. It seemed that with the windows of Haywire closed, exhaust gas leaking into the engine compartment had been pumped between the two windscreens by the heater fan which de-iced them, and thence into the cab. Over a period of days Geoffrey's blood had been increasingly affected, until at last so many corpuscles had been destroyed by the gas that now his life was threatened. We were at 87°59'S and at 10,000 feet, with only enough oxygen to treat him for five hours. Unless he could either be taken quickly down to sea level, or fresh supplies of oxygen procured, there was a grave danger that his heart or brain might be permanently damaged. I immediately signalled to Ed Hillary asking him to approach Admiral Dufek to see if one of the long-range American Neptunes from McMurdo Sound could fly to our assistance.

While Ralph Lenton was trying to break in on one of the radio schedules and pass the message, we continued with the seismic shot. Allan Rogers, who was familiar with electronic equipment, undertook to work the recording apparatus. Breathing pure oxygen, Geoffrey was by now beginning to feel better and bravely insisted on being carried out on a stretcher to Haywire, where he was laid on the floor. There, without needing to move, he could tell Allan the correct sequence of actions to operate the various instruments. After the firing, George Lowe developed the record, while Hal Lister read the gravimeter. In this way Geoffrey still managed to carry out his work, and we continued our journey with the patient lying in the back of County of Kent, where there was more room than in the other vehicles.

At eight o'clock that evening two Neptune planes took off from McMurdo Sound bringing us additional supplies of oxygen. By the time they reached us the sky was completely overcast, with cloud lying only eight hundred feet above the surface, and it was felt that the risk of landing was too great now that Geoffrey's condition no longer appeared to be immediately dangerous. The pilots therefore parachuted oxygen bottles and breathing apparatus from the aircraft. While we collected the equipment they circled above us until we could say that nothing had been damaged in the drop, then they flew away on their 800-mile return trip. Soon Geoffrey was receiving pure oxygen every three hours, with many further hours at a strength equivalent to the atmosphere at sea level. Thanks to the Americans we had no further worries about his condition, and three days later Allan allowed him to resume his work.

All the next day we travelled over sastrugi, but fortunately this time they were directed along the line of our course—quite a change after so many hundreds of miles before the Pole when they had always lain across our track. After fifty-five miles Wrack & Ruin's engine gave trouble and she had to be towed into camp. At this high altitude the Weasel had suffered badly, and now that we had sufficiently reduced our loads we did not really need her any more. So, in latitude 87°01'S, longitude 141°00'E, she was abandoned, and George Lowe, who had endured her shortcomings for so long, thankfully transferred all his photographic equipment to Haywire, where he was to ride for the rest of the journey.

The 30th January was a maintenance day, but on the 31st we travelled seventy miles—a record run for the journey so far, and the first occasion since long before reaching the Pole when we had been able to drive in top gear. After fifty-one miles Roy reported that the outer main bearing of one of his pontoons had broken up, and would have to be replaced. This was the first of a series of different Sno-Cat troubles that now began to haunt us. By the evening of the 4th we had moved forward another 108 miles, but one after the other the tracks on the 'cats' had begun to give trouble. They had gradually become looser, until a point was reached when they repeatedly jumped the lower guide rail and jammed solid with a nasty jarring noise. To tighten all four tracks of one Sno-Cat, 592 steel links had to be bent by hand with a special tool—a long job, taking at least an hour for each track and requiring considerable judgement, for it was essential to make, by eye, an equal adjustment all round and yet arrive at the correct degree of tension at the end The fact that there was no means of bending the links back if one should go too far, tended to make the operator over careful, and he would end his task only to find that the track was still too loose. Then the whole process would have to be begun all over again.

The 4th being a maintenance day, nearly all the track tensioning was completed. In addition, the normal tasks of greasing 296 points on the tracks of each 'cat' and the topping up of the two gearboxes and two differentials were carried out. All this was an unpleasant 'chore' with the temperature at −20°F and the wind blowing at twenty knots. Most of us kept an old pair of gloves and windproofs for this work because filling grease guns was a slimy, slippery process, and the waste grease exuding from the nipples in thin, worm-like threads, blew about in the wind, to become mixed with snow, and finally to stick to the unfortunate who was humping his way to and fro, like a seal, between the tracks.

The trials of maintenance day were added to on this occasion by the discovery that the main steering attachment for the front pontoons was loose on three of the 'cats'. Metal locking tags had therefore to be made, like one already fitted to Rock 'n Roll. As a result of all this work we did not start to travel until half-past eight that night, and again we did not crawl into our sleeping bags until four o'clock in the morning—but we had added thirty-three miles to our total mileage.

Now we were approaching the area where Ed Hillary had reported numerous crevasses and we began to keep a sharp look out. For a time it seemed that we had by-passed the first of these zones, but then they suddenly appeared and Rock 'n Roll halted a few feet in front of a crevasse. For a thousand miles we had been free of these pitfalls; now, as we approached the area where the great ice sheet begins to descend between the mountains on this other side of the continent, the movement of the ice was breaking up the surface and we should have to be very careful. At this stage, having come so far in safety, it seemed a very silly time to come to grief, and we began to look upon the crevasses with an almost personal animosity.

The first of these new crevassed areas was two and a half miles across and was composed of fifty parallel crevasses up to seventy-five feet wide, extending many miles on either side of our course. Fortunately they proved to be very strongly bridged and gave us no trouble. In the remaining fifty miles to Depot 700 there was only one more crevassed stretch but this was more difficult to cross. Twice, Sno-Cats broke through but bounded out of the crevasse leaving eight-foot-wide holes behind them. One 'cat' suffered severe damage but was repaired by Roy Homard and Ralph Lenton. At one time we travelled seven miles alongside a crevasse until, winding from one crossing point to another, Rock 'n Roll and County of Kent could find a way over it, and reach clear ground, with only twenty-seven miles to go to reach the depot.

Behind, Haywire and Able were halted to make repairs to the steering of Able, damaged by the rough going. At intervals they reported how they were getting on by radio, while we pressed on to establish the route all the way to the depot. Shortly before nine on the evening of 7th February, we saw Depot 700 three miles ahead, and half an hour later drew up beside the tall mast and waving marker flag.

Over the radio we heard that down at Scott Base there was whiteout and falling snow, making it impossible for Ed Hillary to fulfil his intention of flying to us, but that he would do so the moment the weather cleared.

Late that night David Pratt and Allan Rogers arrived to fetch another spare steering pin for Haywire, which had now suffered exactly the same damage as her companion Able only a few miles before. All the next day we waited. Repairs to the 'cat' were still going on and the weather at Scott Base remained too bad for flying. David Pratt had gone back to the damaged vehicle by himself, leaving Allan with us, so he was able to attend to a tooth of mine which had been giving considerable trouble ever since we had left the Pole.

Dentistry in a small pyramid tent is necessarily a primitive operation, the patient lying with his head on a box, or between the dentist's knees, the latter's legs doubled up beneath him, and instruments inconveniently placed in precarious positions. At least on this occasion Allan had the advantage of electric light powered from one of the 'cats' and he did an excellent job and relieved me of much pain.

During the day 405 gallons of petrol were pumped into our tanks and empty drums, and extra food supplies were loaded on to the sledges. At half-past ten in the evening of the 9th Able and Haywire arrived at last, and three-quarters of an hour later the Beaver, piloted by John Claydon, brought in Ed Hillary to join our party.

After the first greetings and the unloading of the plane, we began refuelling the newly arrived 'cats' and the Beaver. Besides mail, they had brought us some eggs and fruit which rapidly froze solid. The eggs would be none the worse, but it was almost an engineering problem to thaw the apples and oranges sufficiently to eat them!

Next morning we were up at eight o'clock after five hours' sleep, and at ten o'clock the convoy moved off, Ed joining David Stratton, Hal Lister and myself in Rock 'n Roll. But we had travelled only eleven miles when we suddenly broke through a six-foot-wide crevasse lid invisible on the surface: clearly it was time to prospect ahead once more. While David drove, Hal, Ed and I ski-ed forward probing for trouble and found innumerable crevasses, many of them twenty to fifty feet across. The zone covered two and a half miles and many diversions were necessary before we won clear.

Meanwhile Able had broken a rear spring—the only one to break throughout the journey. David Pratt replaced this while the rest of us were feeling our way slowly forward, and soon we found Ed's old tractor trail and followed it for mile after mile, over undulation after undulation, until we camped by an old snow cairn left by one of the Scott Base dog sledge parties.

Next day Able again fell behind in the first twenty miles. If vehicles became isolated it was our practice to 'listen out' on our radio sets every hour and soon we heard David Pratt calling us to say that poor Able was once more in trouble—this time with a fractured weld of the main steering cross-bar. This meant that Roy Homard and Ralph Lenton in County of Kent had to go back with the spare they were carrying. Three hours later, as we grew colder and colder waiting in our vehicles, we heard that the repair was going well and David urged us to go on.

Soon we were descending into a valley, and near the bottom we came upon the Weasel Ed had abandoned on his way south two months earlier. Had we been in need of another vehicle we could now have repaired it, but the Sno-Cats were doing well, so we pushed on to Midway Depot and pitched our camp. Presently County of Kent was on the air to us and we heard that having repaired the steering, they had only travelled five miles when Able's main transmission-box had broken up and they had been forced to stop again to fit a spare—another long and laborious task with the temperature still at $-20°F$. We ourselves had by now finished the seismic work so we took advantage of the rare opportunity to catch up some of our lost sleep until, during the afternoon, County of Kent and Able lumbered up to us out of the drift.

Two days later, while travelling over very rough and hummocky surface, I found it increasingly difficult to steer. While I was wondering at this, Rock 'n Roll took charge and described an S bend over which I had no apparent control. On climbing out I could see that the front and rear pontoons were pointing in quite different directions, an unwanted condition we traced back to the same welds giving way as had failed on Able. Having used our last spares, the broken parts would have to be rewelded.

We pitched our camp and began to dismantle the steering. As an insurance, the engineers inspected the same welds on the other 'cats', and found that the break had gone almost as far on Haywire although it had not yet affected the steering. Now our special Terylene tent for work on the vehicles really came into its own—indeed without it we could never have done these repairs, for there was a brisk breeze and the temperature had fallen to $-38°F$. With seventy degrees of frost to contend with, it was essential to do the pre-heating and prolonged cooling of the heavy metal parts under cover, while, for the actual electric welding, it was equally important. This pre-heating and after-cooling was carried out with blow torches over a period of some hours, and it was half-past five in the morning before the two Davids, Roy, and Jon Stephenson climbed wearily into their sleeping bags. Even then the job was not completed—it took all the next day to finish the welding and reassemble the 'cats'.

At last, on 17th February, we got away again, to cover the remaining sixty-three miles to Depot 480. As we approached, the depot was clearly visible from a distance of four miles, and soon we could pick out the flanking cairns, gleaming white in the sun on either side. Here we picked up more fuel, lubricating oils, grease and food.

We left the next day in a complete whiteout. Unable to use our sun compasses and with no possibility of seeing anything in front, I was driving with my eyes fixed firmly on the magnetic compass. Suddenly David Stratton nudged me and pointed ahead. There were three Sno-Cats coming towards us! We had entered an area where the magnetic compass was so sluggish that it would not respond, and by following it I had unknowingly turned completely round and was heading straight back towards the South Pole. Halting the others, we experimented several times, always with similar results; then, realizing that we should make no progress in this way we sought other means of keeping our course.

The first scheme to be tried was a method by which four of us ski-ed ahead carrying bundles of trail flags. Starting with three sticks carefully orientated by a prismatic compass which had been allowed to steady for a long time, we would plant one flag after another in line with the first three, at intervals of two hundred yards and thereby extend the original line of the route. The vehicles then followed the flags, a man on the last sledge picking them up for use farther on. After some miles we found this both slow and very hard work.

We next devised a method by which the markers were placed alternately by two men riding on the sledges of the leading vehicle and picked up by the men on the sledge behind the last. The problem then was for the leading driver to maintain a more or less straight course, for it was impossible for him to see behind. This was accomplished by Ed standing on the front seat of Rock 'n Roll, with his head and shoulders through the escape hatch, facing backwards, and calling 'left' or 'right' to the driver. Although it was very cold work, we travelled another fifteen miles in the right direction; but it was still too slow.

The following day we still had whiteout and flagging had to continue. This time the method was modified so that the driver looked backwards out of the open door while steering with his right hand behind him, forward vision and accelerator control being provided by the passenger. This certainly speeded things up, but the strain on the driver's arms and neck was considerable, especially as his left hand had constantly to grip the window frame to ensure that the lurching of the Sno-Cat did not precipitate him through the open door and beneath the rear tracks of his vehicle. By changing drivers every two hours we managed to move forty-two miles in the day, and were glad to feel that at last we had found a way in which we could travel satisfactorily in a whiteout.

So it went on; maintenance on the 20th, followed by twenty-five miles of more route-flagging, and another thirty-nine miles flagged on the 21st as the whiteout persisted. Relief came next day when slight visibility made it possible to see surface irregularities, and for fifteen miles we went 'sastrugi hopping'—that is, driving from one selected ridge to the next and maintaining a reasonable course.

Distant rocky mountains were now just visible over the snow horizon—the first rock we had seen since leaving the Whichaway Nunataks in December. On 23rd February the forward steering arm of Haywire dropped, and, catching in the snow, buckled back under the vehicle to be completely destroyed. The fitting of a spare took some hours, but by the evening we had all reached Plateau Depot at 8,275 feet, only a few miles from the head of the Skelton Glacier.

The airmen at Scott Base had been following our progress over the radio and just as we were pitching our tents after digging out the fuel drums and ration boxes, there was a roar of engines overhead as both the Otter and the Beaver flew low over the depot to circle and land beside us. As the temperature was—30°F both engines were kept running while we exchanged greetings with the two Johns who were piloting the planes, and Wally Tarr who had 'come for the ride'. After loading some superfluous material from the depot into the aircraft, a brief 'party' took place inside the fuselage of the Otter where fourteen of us congregated to share the bottles of beer that John Lewis had thoughtfully brought with him, while we shouted vociferously at each other over the noise of the engines!

Soon the planes took off again and that night we laid out the seismic gear for the final shot. As the task was completed the sun disappeared for the first time beneath the southern horizon—a reminder that the season was drawing to a close and it was time to leave the high plateau. With the clouds lit red by the hidden sun, and the snow mauve in semi-shadow, yet flecked by darker colours in every hollow, we walked to our tents, knowing that the next day we should plunge over the edge of the plateau and wind our way down through the unfamiliar scene of rocky mountains and towering cliffs.

On the 24th, when the seismic work was at last complete, we entered the wide area which the Ross Sea Party had named 'The Portal', and began the long descent of the Skelton Glacier. Within a few miles the sky clouded over, the guiding rocks were hidden from view by drift, and we began again to flag our route—Ed's tall figure planting the markers one after the other in an invisible surface, while I hung out of the open door of Rock 'n Roll, my neck twisted round, my left hand grasping the window frame and my right the wheel. Soon the following wind began to fill the cab with snow, and I found the cold too great to endure the necessarily cramped and twisted driving position. When we stopped to camp after only fifteen miles, the wind speed was found to be thirty knots and the temperature —38°F.

Next day conditions improved and we covered fifty-two miles, descending the Upper Staircase, over the Landing and down the Lower Staircase in brilliant sunny weather. Towards evening the wind rose again, and before we could pitch our camp it was gusting to over fifty knots. Using the vehicles as windbreaks we managed to erect the tents, but all night the poles were bending ominously and we listened to the constant noisy flapping of the canvas.

The following morning camp was broken in thick drift with the wind blowing at thirty-five knots. As we ran down the steeper inclines we found them so smooth and hard that the sledges slid wildly from side to side, completely out of control.

184

Those linked to a 'cat' by a solid bar came to no harm, but Roy's sledges were on steel wire tows, which allowed them to slide right into County of Kent, crashing against the rear pontoons and again damaging the broken steering platform. At the same time a solid wooden beam carried on top of the front sledge pierced the rear door of the 'cat', nearly transfixing those inside.

185

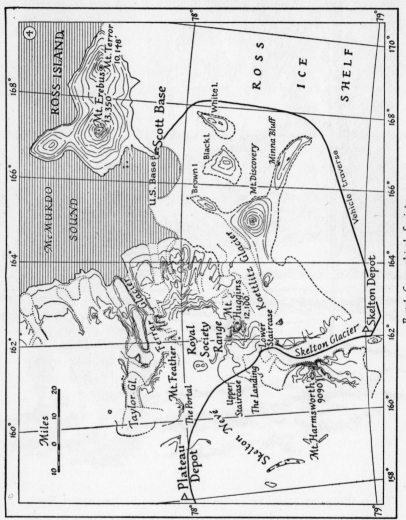

Royal Geographical Society

After this escape, and when the repairs were completed, Roy used a heavy rope brake under the sledge runners to help him reach the bottom of the slope in safety.

Here, in particular, Ed's first-hand knowledge of the route now saved us many hours, and soon we reached the Skelton Depot on the Ross Ice Shelf. That night we climbed into our sleeping bags at a quarter-past four in the morning, knowing that now there remained but 180 miles of level travelling over the ice shelf between us and Scott Base.

The 27th was our last day of maintenance. It would be some time before any of us would have to fill a grease gun again, or flounder between the pontoons covered in a sticky mixture of oil and drift. All the depot stores were dug out so that we could choose those which we hoped later to fly back to Scott Base instead of leaving them to be lost in the field. These we carried with us for the twenty miles travelled that evening, for the surface near the depot was too rough for the planes to land.

The next day, after the aircraft had picked up this extra load, we covered a further sixty-five miles uneventfully, but on the morning of 1st March, just as we were setting off, the 'Antarctic traffic accident' that everyone had joked about as a remote possibility for two years, actually happened. We saw an American Otter flying towards us and as it circled the vehicles, we exuberantly fired a 'two star red' firework as a gesture of *joie de vivre*. The American pilot took this to mean that we needed something, so he made a circuit and came in to land. Looking back from Rock 'n Roll I saw the plane touch down and told David Stratton, who was driving, to stop. In a moment the following 'cat', whose driver and passengers were also looking behind them at the aircraft, began to climb up over the top of our rear sledge! When we examined the damage we found that not only was the sledge wheel completely destroyed, but a box containing many hundreds of detonators had been smashed into small splinters and the metal containers were themselves crushed almost flat. Had they exploded, it certainly would have been the end of the climbing Sno-Cat. Gingerly, at the end of a *very* long rope, we towed the 'cat' slowly backwards off the sledge without further trouble. In all the excitement we forgot about the plane, which had taxied across the snow only to take off again without stopping!

Once we got going again we made the longest run of the whole journey, travelling seventy-five miles by the time we camped and leaving only twenty-two miles to go to Scott Base. Before starting next morning—2nd March—we decorated the Sno-Cats for the last time with all the available flags and headed off towards Castle Rock, where we had been told that we should find a fuel drum marking the beginning of a prepared route through the pressure ridges near the base.

As we ran in towards the island, the huts at Scott Base became visible against the dark rock of Pram Point. Presently there were signs of excitement at the base and we saw Weasels, Ferguson tractors and Bren-gun carriers streaming out along the track to meet us. Soon we joined up, and as the Sno-Cats thundered and weaved between the ridges, escorted in front and behind by every sort of vehicle, for all the world like four battleships with an attendance of excited destroyers, scores of figures stood camera in hand at every vantage point.

When finally we drew up at Scott Base we had travelled 2,158 statute miles from Shackleton, via the South Pole. The journey had been estimated to take a hundred days at an average speed of twenty miles per day. We now found that the trip had lasted ninety-nine days (ninety-eight if it is remembered that we crossed the date line at the Pole), and we had averaged twenty-two miles per day.

As the four Sno-Cats drew up on the sea ice in front of Scott Base, we received a great welcome. Confusion reigned as scores of photographers had their way with the somewhat astonished new arrivals. Then we all congregated around the flagstaff and listened to speeches from our own people and the Americans. An improvised band from the American base 'over the hill' did their enthusiastic worst with our national airs, ending up with what we were told was meant to be *God Save the Queen*. The band had only been formed the night before when the base commander had called for all who could play an instrument. The edict had gone forth: 'It doesn't matter if you can't play—but you gotta be able to play loud!'—and they certainly did!

At last we were taken inside the hut, still talking and laughing —it was good to be able to wash and shave again and to enjoy the feel of clean clothing. All sense of tiredness had vanished and it was—as usual—very late that night when we went to bed!

On 5th March 1958 we sailed north in H.M.N.Z.S. *Endeavour* over the ice-free waters of McMurdo Sound. Twelve days later, in brilliant sunshine, we sailed into Wellington Harbour. By chance the *Magga Dan* had arrived a few days before and we were delighted to see her red-painted hull coming out to meet us early in the morning, carrying our families and friends. We were given a noisy welcome by the ships lying in the harbour and a flight of R.N.Z.A.F. Vampires that screamed overhead—an unforgettable reception by the hospitable people of New Zealand.

This was the end of the Expedition as the public saw it. The three-year programme had been completed. We had crossed the almost unknown continent of Antarctica from one side to the other via the South Pole, conducting our scientific schedule as we had planned. But for us it was only the beginning of a new endeavour, for now we must produce the results from our observations which alone will justify the support we received, and help to give us a better understanding of the world in which we live.

We all hope that the thousands of young people who took such a keen interest in our fortunes, and to whom this book is dedicated, will feel a personal satisfaction that our Antarctic Adventure was a success, and that the Expedition achieved that which it had set out to do.